Other books by Carole Golder
published by Henry Holt

Moon Signs for Lovers
The Seductive Art of Astrology
Love Lives

Carole Golder's

Star Signs

★ ★ ★ ★ ★ ★ ★ ★ ★

AN ASTROLOGICAL GUIDE
TO THE INNER YOU

AN OWL BOOK

★

Henry Holt and Company
New York

Henry Holt and Company, Inc.
Publishers since 1866
115 West 18th Street
New York, New York 10011

Henry Holt® is a registered trademark
of Henry Holt and Company, Inc.

Library of Congress Cataloging-in-Publication Data
Golder, Carole.
[Star signs]
Carole Golder's star signs : an astrological guide to the inner you.
p.   cm.
"An Owl book."
1. Astrology.   2. Zodiac.   I. Title.
BF1726.G65   1994   94-10357
133.5'2—dc20   CIP

ISBN 0-8050-3239-8 (pbk.)

Henry Holt books are available for special
promotions and premiums. For details contact:
Director, Special Markets.

First published in Great Britain in 1993
by Judy Piatkus (Publishers) Ltd.

First Owl Book Edition—1994

Designed by Sue Ryall

Illustrations by Hanife Hassan O'Keeffe

Printed in the United States of America
All first editions are printed on acid-free paper.∞

1   3   5   7   9   10   8   6   4   2

Dedication

I'd like to dedicate this book to my Leo soulmate, Peter Prins.

I also want to thank Judy Piatkus and Gill Cormode for making this my fourth book for them; and to thank my many friends, including Oskarr, all over the world for being such an important part of my life and for being such special people – all of them.

I hope that getting in touch with the Inner You helps to make the world a better place for everyone!

Contents

Carole Golder's
Star Signs

The Inner You

———— ☆ ————

This book is more than just a guide to your outer star sign personality, it also delves beneath the surface. You will recognise some of your characteristics straight away, but others may be far less apparent. Most people enjoy identifying themselves, even if they don't necessarily own up to some of the descriptions associated with them, and now you can take this one step further. You can discover the inner personality of your star sign. This side of your star sign can be a revelation!

I have become especially interested in this inner personality because recently my clients seem to have much more on their minds than material issues such as money, jobs and their love lives. These are naturally still important to them, but they want to discuss other issues too. These relate to their inner feelings.

I am being asked more and more about how we can get in touch with our inner selves and grow spiritually. I want my new book to show not only the outer personality of each star sign, but the inner one too. I hope that by recognising and understanding your own deepest strengths and weaknesses you are better able to deal with life.

These days we are all aware that we're living in a world which is undergoing diverse and often turbulent changes. We are coming to realise that the importance we have placed on materialism seems to have led to an upsurge of greed, corruption, war, famine, drug dependence and crime. We have seen a decline in family values, increasing sexual promiscuity and the onslaught of the HIV virus. Far from bringing an increase of riches, this materialistic outlook on life has only increased the problems in the world. More and more people are feeling unhappy, insecure and disillusioned with their lives.

The world we live in affects us deeply, and we can't afford to ignore the feelings and uncertainties it produces within us. People are now wanting to know '*Why* am I the way I am?' and 'how can I get to know *me* better?' Many clients are saying to me, 'I feel deep down inside that there has to be more to life, and I'm not doing enough about it.'

I'm sure this isn't just a passing phase. We are on the threshold of the Age of Aquarius and in some ways it's as though we're in a deep void, the void between the world as we have known it and the threshold of something new, something of which we have no experience and which we therefore sometimes fear or doubt. We cannot accurately predict what the future holds and it's difficult to feel excited or positive about what is in front of us when we are riddled with doubt and fear.

I feel that with all the changes that have been taking place over the years, we can no longer rely on our outer personalities – no matter what Ascendant we possess or where all the different planets are placed in our charts – to get us through the positives and negatives of life. I strongly believe in the ability of our Inner Self to help guide us in the right direction and into the New Age. Whatever uncertainties there may be, there are signs that this Age will be one of greater spirituality. Now is an ideal time to get in touch with your inner you.

In this book, therefore, I want to show you how to recognise and understand your own deepest strengths and weaknesses so that you are better able to deal with the changes taking place throughout the world. By learning to balance mind, body and soul, and by growing stronger within, we can help to make that world a more positive place and look forward with confidence to what the future may bring.

When you take an inner look at yourself, at that often hidden side of your star sign personality, you really can know who you are and where you need to go. And when you learn more about yourself, you can learn a lot more about others too. That's what this book is all about.

It would be so wonderful to be able to wave a magic wand over the world, to know that the ozone layer would repair itself, that natural disasters would no longer occur and that wars, famines and incurable illnesses would be things of the past. Unfortunately most of us can only do a very small amount to help the world as a whole, but we can do something that will make a difference to the quality of our lives and the lives of those around us. This, in turn, will have a knock-on effect in a wider sense. What we can do is get to know ourselves as no one else knows us. By becoming more aware of our innermost needs, hopes and desires, we can learn to deal with the stressful lifestyle of the 1990s which can take such a great toll on all our lives. We will become far more in tune with ourselves in mind, body and spirit, and far less difficult to live with.

I want to show you how your Zodiac personality is the key to reaching the innermost part of your character. Within each and every one of us is an Inner Being. I've always thought of this inner being as a little child, sometimes a little child eager to learn, sometimes one who feels they know everything already, sometimes one who holds on to fear, or to old routines and regimes out of stubbornness or a refusal to change. The whole point about this little child is that it needs to feel loved, secure, confident and strong. Isn't that just how you want to feel too, no matter what your sign? Your little child within is someone with exactly the same star sign as the rest of you, and each star sign chapter in this book has its own meditation and affirmation to help you to get to know your inner self better and love yourself more.

It has been wonderful for me, while writing this book, to come to a better understanding not just of myself, but of all the people closest to me. I can understand the insecurity lurking below the surface of a seemingly self-sufficient Taurus; I know the reasons for that Virgo being *so* self-critical, and why, because that particular Libra made some faulty decisions in the past, he or she still hesitates over certain situations today. It's been fun checking out the vulnerability hiding within a bossy old Leo, and pointing out to Aries that patience really can bring rewards, all in the right time.

Worldwide, so many things have changed in the last year while I have been writing this book. In England, the House of Windsor has been shaken by the scandals surrounding the marriage problems of the Prince and Princess of Wales and the Duke and Duchess of York. In the USA, a young, positive and enthusiastic presidential candidate survived scandals in his personal life to win the election. In Germany there are appalling conflicts between those people involved in the upsurge of Neo-Fascism and those continually working for peace. Yugoslavia has been torn apart; the photographs of people dying in Somalia have broken all our hearts; at the time of writing, Saddam Hussein continues to make headlines. Yet, there are definite rays of hope and at least the threat of nuclear war has become a little less with the signing of the Start II treaty between Russia and America. In any event, we must all go on with a more positive approach to life and the world. What better way to start than by knowing ourselves a little better?

Maybe we have to go down to the depths in order to come up again triumphant, just like the Phoenix rising from the ashes. I'm sure that being truly positive and balanced in mind, body and soul will create an inner strength which cannot be shaken.

Remember that you don't have to look any further than inside you!

Aries

─────── ☆ ───────

MARCH 21 – APRIL 20

Aries is the first sign of the Zodiac, relating to the first day of the Spring equinox. You are a Masculine, Cardinal, Positive sign, the first of the Fire signs. Mars, God of War, is your planetary ruler, and your planetary symbol is the Ram.

An enthusiastic, enterprising, dynamic and pioneering leader, that's you – with masses of energy, initiative and vitality. No challenge is too great for you, no worthwhile cause undeserving of your support.

You love excitement and adventure, and are extremely passionate and emotional. Your zest for life, your sense of humour and that boundless energy will always attract people to your side, even if your impatience has in the past often exhausted them too. However, people who may hold a grudge against you could also criticise you for being too outwardly aggressive, fiery, impatient and quick-tempered, a daredevil with hardly a thought for anyone or anything other than your own desires. Since unabashed honesty is also one of your attributes, you may feel inclined to admit that on bad days this can indeed be true!

Aries rules the head, so it's not surprising that adjectives like 'headstrong' and 'headlong' are often associated with you. With the typical Aries, everything has to be done 'yesterday'. You invariably exhaust yourself, let alone everyone who comes in contact with you. You also have a terrible habit of rushing headlong into relationships, projects, and probably brick walls too, without bothering to use your Aries head to look before you leap! You're so determined to make your mark upon the world in one way or another that sometimes this can be a real problem – you don't stand still long enough to know in which way you *do* want to make that mark!

Obviously, in any astrology book one can only generalise. Perhaps your own personal horoscope contains so many diverse planetary aspects that your Aries personality is overshadowed and it is hard to guess you *are* an Aries. But that is simply guess-work, and it is unlikely.

However, by starting to take more of an interest in the inner parts of your psyche, instead of being so concerned with what is happening on the surface – that is, by discovering what lies beneath your ego – you will find even more excitement and adventure, together with much more enjoyment, in your everyday life. Sometimes you are simply too concerned with ego: it's almost as if you came into the world crying 'me first'.

What you usually need, more than almost anything else in your life, is a challenge. Discovering and getting to know your inner personality can be your very own personal challenge for the future, something to be tackled with your customary enthusiasm and idealism. Think how wonderful it will be to find a way to be more patient, less aggressive, and more understanding of other people's priorities without losing complete sight of your own. While the Outer You is continually thinking and saying 'me first', the Inner You will teach you to calmly accept that there are times when this is simply not a feasible situation.

This is where you will face a problem almost all Ariens are certain to recognise, for discovering what is really behind that firebrand personality is not something that usually happens overnight. Far from it. No matter how highly evolved you may consider yourself already through different teachings or tech-niques, the very first stumbling block is bound to be something very simple. It is usually one little word: patience.

If patience is something you do happen to be endowed with, you are indeed a very rare Aries. It probably means that your own personal horoscope contains not only an Ascendant and Moon which make you patience personified, but a plethora of brilliant planetary aspects which add to these. It's one of the hardest things in the world for a typical Aries to feel that they have the necessary time available to wait for anyone or anything longer than is absolutely necessary. However, it's about time you convinced yourself that patience is a *virtue* and not a sin! Once you've learnt the value of this, you will begin to discover that greater success can result through good timing than through those headstrong, impulsive reactions and decisions of old. And your inner self-confidence will start to increase.

As an Aries, no matter what else is going on in your own personal horoscope, you are possessed with great courage and a wonderful pioneering quality. Therefore, to fulfil your greatest potential and step forward with that little bit extra to give yourself and everyone else, think of this discovery of the Inner You as a new adventure. It may mean having to release or re-format ideas about yourself you've held for years and letting go of any dead wood. You must also be willing to admit that you may have made mistakes in the past through impulsive and impatient decisions. Perhaps this is also the moment to advise you that even a fiery Arien cannot change the world single-handed . . . sometimes you need to accept help and advice from others on your ideas, ideals and projects. Even with Mars, God of War, aiding and abetting you when it is time for you to fight your own personal wars, when you are more in tune with your Inner Self you will start to realise and accept that some issues *are* bigger than you. It is always easier for a typically courageous Aries to rush right in, but that is when a *different* kind of courage is needed – the courage to hold back and perhaps put whatever is bothering you in the hands of a higher power.

Many of you are extremely idealistic, and without any doubt great romantics. Casanova was an Aries; so is Warren Beatty. Although you revel in the excitement of the chase, the subsequent romantic conquest can fall short of those idealistic expectations. Helter-skelter, you fall head over heels in love, yet often it is purely physical attraction. Where is the mental stimulation and communication that your heart is yearning for? What you are really looking for deep down is a true soulmate!

Sometimes your insistence on trying to conquer the world in twenty-four hours, without taking into account anyone or anything else, really does work against you. You can't *always* have things your own way, like a spoilt child. That 'me first' attitude might have seemed appealing when you were six months old, but it holds you back if you don't let it go as you get older. When you come to understand your Inner Self more, and to appreciate the greater clarity of vision that comes with opening up your mind to its higher potential, you will find it much easier to realise and accept that this is not usually possible. Sometimes you are simply too self-involved for your own good, and can create a feeling in others that you simply don't care about them.

We all have an outer personality and an inner one. And for you, learning to balance your often impetuous, impatient and sometimes needlessly aggressive outer attitude with an inner, more focused awareness and insight into your highest potential could turn you into one of the most important pioneers of the coming century.

Each time you feel yourself behaving in a hasty, thoughtless, impulsive way, take a deep breath – take several in fact – and think about balance. Think about your opposite sign in the Zodiac, Libra (sign of the Scales). Each and every one of us has something important to learn from our opposite sign: it contains some of what is lacking in us. In the same way we have something in our Arien make-up which can help Librans.

Positive and Negative, Yin and Yang, we need both, and with the correct balance a sort of miracle takes place. Our lives can take on a new, enhanced glow. As an Aries, you will discover that being more evolved, more developed in the spiritual sense, doesn't mean you have to set off for the highest peak of the Himalayas to meditate or search for a Guru. Sitting quietly in a comfortable seat in your living room will do just as well if you can quieten your mind sufficiently to listen to the still, silent voice within which can point you in the right direction to achieve your highest potential in your daily life. Later in this chapter you will find your very own meditation technique and affirmation to help you do this. Meanwhile, it will help to think of your inner personality rather as a little child, a little child whose enterprising and free-spirited ways can certainly be encouraged, but who needs also to appreciate the value of patience and good timing.

PATHWAYS TO SUCCESS IN THE 1990s

★ Enjoy the time you spend doing something, and don't always rush to finish it.
★ Believe in yourself, but accept that other people can be right too.
★ Enjoy what life has to offer you without expecting it as your due, or promoting yourself *too* much.
★ It's wonderful to see things through the eyes of a child, but remember that the wisdom of maturity can be a major bonus.
★ Be bold, brave and enthusiastic, but remember that holding back doesn't have to mean you're scared!
★ Balance your energetic ways with the benefit of greater inner peace.

YOUR RULING PLANET . . . Mars, God of War

One of the major influences on a male or female Aries is your planetary ruler. Since Mars, ruler of Aries, was the Roman God of War, perhaps it's no wonder you tend to charge through life as if it was your own personal battlefield; as though Mars himself was controlling your every action, arming you with an invisible spear and shield. No wonder you have that daredevil attitude which rises to every challenge as though there was no tomorrow! Mars relates to passion and energy, sexual drive and creativity, and gives you your Arien strength and courage, but remember that this planet can also make you overly argumentative, competitive and aggressive, and at times accident prone. Happily, your 'Martian energy' is more often expressed through your mind, so that arguments don't normally lead to violence. In the body Mars rules the blood, especially the red corpuscles, and Martian-ruled Ariens are often highly sexed.

In Northern Europe Mars was identified with Tiw, Tyr or Tig. The sign of Tiw was a phallic spear attached to a female disc, and it was as the wielder of that spear of fertility that Mars or Tiw became a god of battle. But that doesn't mean you have to go through life as if there is *always* a personal battle for you. If you start to listen to your inner voice you will begin to believe that there *is* a tomorrow, and that harnessing your Martian energy to your goals in a positive way is far the best means of achieving your long term aims. So hold impatience back by its tail, and allow Mars to inspire you fearlessly in your creative ideas, to stimulate you in following through in your beliefs and ideals, and to endow you with the bravery and courage to overcome any problems you may encounter.

Every Zodiac sign has its own particular colour or colours and red – appropriate to the war-god Mars, your planetary ruler – has been bequeathed to Aries.

In ancient times your planetary symbol, the Ram, was an embodiment of the phallic god and in the first and second centuries BC the ram was used as a religious sacrifice, with his death signifying a rebirth, the ending and beginning of a cycle of life. The ancient Egyptians' Amen-Ra was the Ram of rams, virile and passionate, and the Greeks in turn linked Aries with the Golden Fleece, guarded always by a dragon until it was rescued by Jason. The glyph of Aries represents the Ram's horn; and Aries represents the period of the year when the ram rested after breeding with his ewes.

As an Arien, with Mars as your ruler, red as your colour, and the Ram as your symbol, you have a powerful challenge – the challenge of discovering more about your inner personality, and of sometimes having to fight the Outer You in order to make your subconscious mind be still. And winning this particular battle will ensure that you become calmer, more focused and an even greater trailblazer!

THE INNER CHALLENGE – THE OUTER CHANGE

There are several areas of your life – probably most of them if you're truthful – that don't always run as smoothly as you would like. But don't allow Mars to over-influence you so that too much of your life really *is* a perpetual war zone! The following areas might be your particular battlefields, and the wonderful thing about learning more about your Inner Self in relation to your sign is that you can achieve a great deal more contentment and fulfilment in all of them.

RELATIONSHIPS

When it comes to love, your inner personality is surprisingly different from that somewhat brash, ardent, impulsive and seemingly unbelievably self-confident firebrand who rushes into each and every relationship without ever thinking you could be turned down by the object of your affections, and whose Martian sexual passion inevitably seems to be both uninhibited and unabated when you are embarked on a romantic chase.

It is sometimes difficult for anyone involved with you to realise that under the surface there is a child-like vulnerability and insecurity that you manage to hide very well. This child-like sensitivity will remain with you throughout your life. It's not just romantic Pisces who puts on those rose-coloured spectacles in order to see the world in a more romantic hue: you do it too. But somehow your Outer You has trained you to consider such behaviour a weakness.

The Inner Aries wants love to be all sweetness and light. You want to be loved and give love with an abundance of passion, and with plenty of romantic and tender words and gestures too.

But so often you ignore this inner part of you and what it needs. Helter-skelter, you go gaily into the chase determined to sweep someone off their feet. You allow that initial chemistry or physical attraction – call it what you will – to drive you on. That Aries warrior is off again! Why don't you start to think more about what your heart and soul are yearning for – a real soulmate relationship, with perfect mental stimulation, communication *and* physical passion – instead of allowing that Outer You to take control? Warren Beatty was once a perfect example of the first part of this description, and now it seems he has discovered the beauty of the second with Annette Bening.

The following guide will help you to see the benefits of getting to know the Inner You when romance is involved.

The Outer You   is challenged by another Aries trailblazer; is frustrated by slow-moving Taurus; is mentally stimulated by Gemini; is put off by Cancer's moods; admires the flamboyance of Leo; dislikes to be criticised by Virgo; is impatient with the indecision of Libra; is passionately attracted to sexy Scorpio; is happy with a Sagittarius who doesn't know *all* the answers; finds Capricorn rather staid and practical; is challenged again by unpredictable Aquarius; wonders whether Pisces is just too, too emotional.

The Inner You   sees below the surface of the Aries firebrand personality; appreciates the emotional security which Taurus gives; will make sure Gemini never feels bored; understands the sentimentality of Cancer; realises why Leo likes to be the centre of attention; understands Virgo is being critical for your own good; appreciates Libra's sense of balance; realises that Scorpio is searching for more than sex; accepts that Sagittarius just loves to be a teacher; understands Capricorn's need for earthbound security; never tries to make Aquarius feel hemmed in; revels in romantic bliss with Pisces.

By delving deeper into your inner being you will find it much easier to recognise and respect what you need out of a romantic relationship in order for it to be successful. You need to feel free and yet can be extremely jealous of anyone with whom you are involved. Inner self-development will help you to find greater self-confidence and to love yourself more – not your outer persona, but the Inner You. You will begin to appreciate the joy of a lasting relationship rather than just its early excitement.

Once you have really developed your own particular way to be more in touch with your Inner Self, you will discover that you can have a much more relaxed relationship with family, friends and the people you work with too.

CAREERS AND BUSINESS

Both male and female Ariens are natural leaders. You don't take too kindly to receiving orders, let alone criticism, from those whose ideas you do not respect.

You are brilliant at starting new ventures, if they are something you firmly believe in. But you can be equally brilliant at losing interest once the initial ideas begin to pall! Perhaps you start to wonder what you have taken on, and how long it may take to pull off this or that project. This is where the understanding of your inner psyche can be invaluable. Martian energy and enthusiasm are simply not enough. The ability to go within will enable you to analyse your deepest thoughts and feelings about a situation or an idea and project an air of calmness and confidence. This will gain you greater respect from your colleagues and make you a real winner.

Arien success is often self-made. John Major and David Frost are two good examples. Jeffrey Archer, Stephen Sondheim, Emma Thompson, Diana Ross, Elton John and Sir John Gielgud were also born under your sign. In career or business issues you put so much into everything you do that you can feel angry and frustrated if you do not fulfil your desires.

The key is to develop your inner strength by understanding that the power of those quiet moments when your mind isn't rushing around in turmoil is as important as any Martian warrior's pre-battle manoeuvres. The greater your inner calm and conviction, the greater will be your own success. Peace *can* bring you power, Aries, and understatement can bring you greater victories. In the coming Age of Aquarius it will be the combination of your whole mind, body and spirit personality that will make you invincible in the career and business stakes.

An additional bonus will be your ability to recognise whether it is your ego which is striving for a certain career position, or whether it is something you are truly meant to do. However, you will almost certainly gravitate to the same types of career –

something in which you can demonstrate your powers of leadership. If you do have to take a subordinate position you will need to work for someone you respect. Ariens are great on deadlines, can cope with crises, and certainly thrive on challenge – but sometimes you have much to learn about teamwork, which is such an important part of life and essential in business.

Your positive powerhouse of energy can be put to fantastic use in the fields of advertising, public relations, journalism, broadcasting, television and politics. Other careers often suggested for you include psychology, dentistry, being a butcher or fireman, and becoming an explorer or professional sportsman or woman.

How Do You Handle Decisions?

Life is full of decisions, and no doubt one of your greatest faults is that you often make them much, much too quickly. And if you are completely honest with yourself you may also have to admit that you sometimes regret them later on.

I realise that you would not want to become the sort of dithery, indecisive person for whom you have no patience at all, but one of the most important lessons you can learn from this guide is that you can achieve much more in life if you evaluate each and every decision you make just that little bit more. I'm not denying that you may have great intuition, or that very often your first instinct over a 'yes' or 'no' is right. I'm simply advising you to slow down and calmly allow your inner voice to have its say.

How can it do that if the Outer You is behaving in an impulsive and impatient way, wanting to know all the answers immediately? The answer is to continue to be a firm decision maker, but don't make 'he who hesitates is lost' your maxim quite so often. In your particular case a few moments of hesitation can bring you a whole wonderland of beneficial results.

How Do You Handle Conflicts?

Learning more about your decision making will in turn help you when it comes to handling conflicts. If you are a typical Aries, I can almost guarantee you that you approach any sort of conflict – whether it be emotional or over a business or domestic issue – just like a battering ram, or like a dog with a bone which he won't let go. Heaven help anyone who tries to pick a fight with a firebrand like you! But can you honestly say you always come out on top, battling forth in your own inimitable way? This is where that knowledge of your Inner You comes into play once again. If you really do know you are right, it's not always necessary to make a song and dance about your beliefs. Don't detract from your inner power, your spiritual strength, by draining your vital energy in unnecessary arguments when there is a chance a peaceful solution can be found. There's a lot to be said for rational and calm discussion rather than hot-headed anger and foot stamping. In times of anger, always try to reach that still silent voice within and listen to its message.

This is an area where your opposite sign of Libra has important knowledge to bequeath you – the art of balance, of seeing two sides of a situation, of weighing up those pros and cons.

Too many dramas have already been played out in the world we live in, and too many dramas have possibly been played out in your own life at one time or another. But if you have begun to value patience, good timing and inner confidence, you won't have to fight so hard in the future.

Peaceful solutions to conflicts may not always be easy, but they are certainly worth aiming for. Your own peace of mind is one of the most important solutions of all.

YOU AS A PARENT

Do you still insist on continuing to be such a whirlwind of energy once you have children of your own? Or have you accepted that your Aries ego really does have to take a back seat once you are responsible for other people?

The beauty of going deeper into your inner being is that your intuition and instincts are heightened to the extent that you won't worry so much about your offspring. In fact you will probably develop a kind of telepathic communication with them.

The one thing you will never lose is your special ability to relate to children in a wonderful way. You will always retain your own individual child-like quality, and this will communicate itself to them. Just make sure that you don't indulge in too much competition with your children as they start to grow up. This applies to both male and female Ariens. It can't always be 'me first', you know!

COPING WITH LIFE AFTER
BREAK-UPS OR BEREAVEMENTS

The more you develop your inner strength, the more you will realise that you are definitely one of the world's survivors. But probably there have also been times in your life when you have been somewhat renowned as a person who is all too fond of dramas! And you may have found that this has worked against you when people think they're having to deal with yet more Aries histrionics.

Coping with break-ups or bereavements is never easy, for any sign, and if you are still hanging on to your old impatient ways, expecting everything to change for the better too quickly, then you are asking for trouble.

This is the time to use your meditation techniques and your affirmation, which you will find on pages 19–20, and to be with the people who understand you best. Be patient, Aries – your warrior's strength will never let you down.

LIFESTYLE, HEALTH AND DIET

The Aries lifestyle is often hard to pin down. You abhor boredom of any kind, and your high energy level can make you hard to keep up with. To bring your outer and inner lives closer together, you may consider the physical and mental well-being which Yoga can bring.

Meditation is one of the best possible ways for someone to still their mind, and it has beneficial effects on the body as a whole. Meditation is not something which can be learnt overnight and invariably needs practice, but once you have mastered it you can move on to other ways which can help to turn even the most impatient Aries into someone who doesn't have to have everything accomplished yesterday! For an Arien about to set forth on this voyage of self-discovery, it is an ideal start. Once you have overcome any early difficulties you will find a new air of tranquillity in your expression.

At the same time, you could have your own personal affirmation, something to say to yourself each morning as regularly as you brush your teeth or wash your face. Devise your own special words which will help you to face each new day with a calmer, more tranquil approach to whatever it may hold and also contain a special message to reach the Inner You. You will find your affirmations at the end of this chapter.

These steps may seem a little unnecessary to you. You see yourself as a leader, not someone who takes orders from others. But these are purely techniques which will enable you to have a much smoother passage on the way to a more fulfilling and contented life. Don't be surprised to become so delighted with your new-found well-being on both the physical and mental planes that you are soon enthusiastically telling your family and friends that they too will enjoy and benefit from discovering more about their own Inner Selves.

Leisure has often seemed almost a dirty word to Ariens, something which is okay for the very young or very old but which has no place in your busy life.

Give yourself a break, Aries, a real break for once. Appreciate those leisure moments which come your way. Enjoy having your weary limbs massaged once in a while. Develop any creative skills which may have lain dormant for years. Take photos on your exciting holiday travel trips. Indulge in some sport which enables you to use up any excess energy in a positive way, but resolve to enjoy yourself even if you don't win that game of tennis or round of golf! Teach yourself greater patience by going fishing; even if you simply accompany someone who is fishing and take a good book along with you, it's a wonderful way to relax (and I'm an Aries who can vouch for that!). Learn about crystals and the benefits of working with them, or spend some invaluable time listening to tapes or reading books by that wonderful Aries, Ram

Dass, whose combination of spiritual wisdom, common sense and humour will inspire you tremendously.

A positive approach to your lifestyle will also help to make you healthier. It's all aligned together – mind, body, spirit. More and more people have been turning to alternative medicine in recent years, and by following this positive approach you will soon discover that a calmer, more tranquil way of life will benefit you in every possible way.

Since, astrologically, Aries rules the head, it may come as no surprise to you that aside from headaches and migraines due to stress and tension in your head area, you may also suffer from nervous exhaustion, insomnia, neuralgia, toothache and problems related to the face in general. You are also prone to cuts, burns and accidents to other parts of your body because you rush around so much without looking where you are going!

A calmer, more tranquil way of eating will benefit a lot of you too. So many Ariens grab hurried meals during the course of the day because you don't consider you have time to sit down and enjoy your food. A well-balanced diet will help to make you well-balanced through and through, something which more and more people are discovering daily. Since you tend to burn up so much energy you do need to replace it, so never skimp on your necessary amount of proteins, or go on a crash diet without obtaining medical advice first.

GROWING OLD GRACEFULLY

The idea of a typical Aries, no matter whether male or female, growing old gracefully is rather amusing. Aries is perhaps the youngest at heart of all the Zodiac signs, and this particular characteristic is unlikely to change. No matter how devoted you become to the understanding of your Inner Self, there is bound to be something within you which is going to rebel at the idea of growing old, gracefully or otherwise. But that's rather wonderful too. As I'm writing this book, I am thinking of one Aries lady who is almost eighty-four years old, and who has just gone off to live in India on her own. While there she rides around on her bicycle and enjoys her life to the full. And 'growing old gracefully' is definitely not a description which she would want to have applied to her, even though her name does happen to be Grace!

But by 'growing old gracefully' I really mean a state of mind: no more rushing into battle, no more dramas, but a real chance to enjoy the pleasures which slowing down a little can bring to your life.

How To Get In Touch With The Inner You

In the introduction to this book I suggested that one way to understand your Inner Self more is to think of it as a little child. As an Aries you're often too tough and rough on that little child, giving it a hard time when you're in a particularly aggressive mood or an impatient frame of mind.

That is why your own particular form of meditation (see page 20) can be such a help for you, and why you must be patient for long enough to overcome those tricky early days when quietening your Aries mind is still a battle.

Of course, you may already have your own way of meditating. That's fine. The important thing is that you recognise the benefits which meditation can bring you.

Then each morning when you are washing and brushing your teeth, look at yourself in the mirror and affirm to yourself with feeling and conviction:

Today I will try harder
to be more patient and understanding

The more you understand your Inner Self, the easier it will be for you to realise that your battling days, while not necessarily completely over *all* the time, will at least have diminished sufficiently to allow you to enjoy your life at a more peaceful pace. You won't have lost your pioneering quality, or your innovative ways, and you'll still be a leader – but a leader who has conquered impatience!

The Aries Meditation

Sit comfortably on the floor in a cross-legged position (or, if this is not comfortable, on a chair). Close your eyes and visualise a beautiful deep red rose opening up. Feel that you can almost breathe in its perfect scent, and imagine that you are completely alone in a wonderful garden, gazing at this rose and inhaling its perfume. Allow your mind to be still but don't worry if thoughts insist on coming in – just let them float by, for all that matters is you and your beautiful rose. Let yourself sink slowly into a meditative state for approximately twenty minutes, at the end of which allow the rose to slowly close again.

Try to do this meditation twice a day. You will soon start to discover a clarity of vision, a calmness, confidence and realisation of your power, plus an inner knowledge that enables you to make daily decisions in a more positive way and at the same time rise above all the day-to-day problems in your life. And don't worry, you will soon know instinctively when twenty minutes are up. Choose a quiet place so that no one can disturb you.

YOUR PERSONAL GUIDE TO THE FUTURE

By following the advice offered in this chapter you will understand and know yourself much better, and in so doing will be able to have even more fulfilling relationships in your emotional and your working life. It is not that you will suddenly change overnight, or give up a job you've always enjoyed to go off and explore the jungle – but you might! What *will* change is your attitude to what you do and the way you follow this through from now on. From being so self-involved, you will become more self*less*.

You won't react irrationally when another star sign disagrees with you, for you will have discovered more about their Inner Self as well as your own. Nothing will seem quite as urgent or such a drama, and you will have learnt something from your opposite sign of Libra and started to see both sides of a situation in a fair and rational way. Sometimes those initial physical attractions could turn into lasting soulmate partnerships if you take the time to get beneath the surface of the Outer You.

Positive Outlooks	Possible Pitfalls
★ Having a more balanced viewpoint	★ Impatience could rear its head again
★ Using your energy more constructively	★ The ego taking too much control
★ Sharing your enthusiasm over your ideals	★ Being unwilling to take advice
★ Enjoying happier relationships	★ Saying you don't *want* to change
★ Becoming more unselfish	★ Going back to a 'me first' attitude
★ Taking pleasure in 'now'	★ *Too* keen on new adventures
★ Becoming more capable of working in partnership	★ Feeling restricted

For the typical Aries, challenge and change will *always* be exciting. The challenge of getting to know and understand the Inner You in order to approach the future in a more positive way will be a wonderful voyage of self-discovery, and it's one challenge you *are* allowed!

Taurus

──── ☆ ────

APRIL 21 – MAY 20

Taurus is the second sign of the Zodiac. You are a Feminine, Fixed, Negative sign, the first of the Earth signs. Venus, Goddess of Love, is your planetary ruler, and your symbol is the Bull.

Practical, persevering, pragmatic and patient, stable and enduring, you are one of those wonderful people who can always be relied upon when problems turn up unexpectedly.

Artistically creative, Barbra Streisand, Glenda Jackson, Candice Bergen, Al Pacino, Cher and Albert Finney are all Taureans. However, some of you sometimes allow your creative flair to lie below the surface of your personality. You may be excellent at waxing forth eloquently about all that you are going to do in life, but you are perfectly content to take second place on too many occasions. Extremely loyal and loving, you tackle whatever has to be done in a responsible and wonderfully calm and placid manner.

In many ways you're a master of strategy; not for you the 'rush in where angels fear to tread' attitude of fiery Aries, the sign which precedes yours in the Zodiac. Even so, in these times of accelerated change in the world it is important to remember that waiting *too* long can sometimes mean you miss the boat and lose out on whatever you are hoping to achieve. Remember too that change can be beneficial, especially if you have gone along in the same old way for too many months or years and are feeling frustrated as a result of this.

Many of you are great romantics, and there is a sensual side to your nature. This may often take a while to come to the surface, but it proves that underneath you can be as passionate as any Scorpio. However, you sometimes set so much importance on your outer needs that you negate your inner need for a soulmate, preferring instead to concentrate on what you consider to be a more realistic and practical partnership.

Obviously, in any astrology book one can only generalise, and your own personal horoscope might contain so many diverse planetary aspects that your Taurus personality is overshadowed and no one would even know you were a Taurus. But that is only speculation, and meanwhile when you start to display the Taurean characteristics of stubbornness and obstinacy, it is only too apparent that you were indeed born under the sign of the Bull!

We all have an outer personality and an inner one. And don't stubbornly refuse to learn more about the Inner You, for it will enable you to understand so much more about the Outer You too. Think of this inner persona rather like a little child, and remember that once that little child feels totally secure on all levels there is no reason why the Outer You need feel insecure, even with all the changes going on around you. Besides, once you discover who you are and what you really want out of life, you will realise that this knowledge can be an incredible benefit. One of the advantages is that you can be completely honest – your Inner Self isn't going to query why you might feel the need for a change, even if you *have* been set in your ways for years.

Taurus is the builder of the Zodiac, born with 'green fingers' and often having the ability to grow even the most difficult plants. With your feet firmly on the ground, you are a true Earth person. So why not start to think of yourself rather like a tree with its roots in the soil, yet growing ever upwards towards the sky? That tree doesn't want to stay close to the ground for it knows the benefit of soaring up to freedom. Why don't you start to think of your Inner Self in the same way? Don't limit yourself by placing so much importance on earthly pleasures that you lose out on what even just a little taste of spiritual involvement can bring you too.

Don't be fearful of discovering more about your true self, or be quite so inflexible, lazy or simply apathetic! Be a little more like your opposite sign in the Zodiac, the invincible Scorpio, for whom knowledge, intuition and curiosity are all elements of power. But remember that while power is something most Taureans greatly respect, it must be treated with care. Too much power is negative, and Taureans such as Hitler, Lucrezia Borgia, Machiavelli, Eva Perón and cult leader Jim Jones were certainly examples of that.

Why not resolve to be less fixed in your opinions and less earthbound in many of your ideas, and start to listen to what the universe is trying to teach you? Learn to become more open and trusting, for the more you do that, the easier you will find it becomes to open up not just to your Inner Self but also to the people with whom you come in contact in your daily life.

To release your maximum potential, be prepared to take a few risks with yourself. Don't continue to go for the tried and true way of doing things but have the courage to fly a little higher. Even if you never imagined before the idea of leaving your own little comfort zone, think how fantastic it will be to feel as much security internally as you insist on striving for in the outer world.

Start to feel more secure in yourself, to like and appreciate yourself more, and at the same time resolve to 'get out there and make life happen', not simply hang back and wait. It's time to create the right balance between your outer and inner personality, and if there are others around who associate your sign with people who can be boring, plodding and need a kick up the backside to get them going, it's time for you to prove them wrong!

A very positive part of your character is that no problem is too great for you to tackle, and no person is too small for you to bother with. Patient, kind and humorous, loving, warm and sensitive, you have a great deal to offer. And when you truly are in tune with your Inner Self you will have even more.

Positive and Negative, black and white, Yin and Yang – all are necessary. The important thing is to find the right balance. For you, the need is to find the right balance between real inner security and the outer security which you appear to achieve with so much ease by seeming so very capable to the rest of us. By honestly accepting yourself for who you are, this will become much easier.

PATHWAYS TO SUCCESS IN THE 1990s

★ Accept that there are some things you *cannot* change, and don't stubbornly try to force them.

★ Don't simply talk about your plans – get out there and create them in reality!

★ Appreciate your innate power to build – to combine your spiritual strength with your outer personality.

★ Remember that everyone has needs and feels insecure at times – but learn to be more secure in yourself by balancing your Inner and Outer personalities and you'll feel more secure with everyone and everything else too.

★ Rest when your work is done – but resolve that you won't be accused of laziness.

YOUR RULING PLANET . . .
Venus, Goddess of Love

One of the major influences on a male or female Taurean is your planetary ruler. You are fortunate, in common with the sign of Libra, to have Venus as yours, for it is she who endows you with a love of beauty, peace and harmony, colour, light and serenity, and a love of love itself. When Venus is your ruling planet – or indeed is strongly aspected in anyone's horoscope – there is almost always a strong attraction to, and talent in, art and music. Venus enables you to smile sweetly at the world, to love and be loved, and she helps to cushion the blows when hurts and disappointments come your way. But be warned, for at the same time Venus can make you lazy, expecting love as your due! And she can accentuate your laid-back Taurean temperament to create a sort of inertia which makes you even less likely to want to change any of your personality, even when you do start to understand the benefits of inner growth. The positive influences of Venus bring your ability to love and your sense of refinement and beauty, while her negative side throws too much emphasis on sensual pleasures! So use the benefits of Venus wisely. Gaze up at her luminous beauty in the night sky and count your blessings that she rules your sign!

In the body, Venus rules the throat, thymus gland and kidneys. Some modern interpretations of classical mythology have portrayed Venus as a sex goddess instead of simply the Goddess of Love, but the Romans associated her with beauty and nature, and her Greek counterpart was the alluring and magnetic Aphrodite. In present day Goddess lore she can also relate to your charisma, the feminine and romantic side of your nature, and to your desire to have the ideal relationship.

In Italy right through to Renaissance times, Venus – the Evening Star – was also known as Stella Maris, the Star of the Sea. Venice was the sacred city of Venus, and on Ascension Day each year the Duke of Venice ceremonially married her by throwing a gold wedding ring into the sea.

Venus was also one of the major goddesses of the Egyptians and Mexicans, and their calendars were based upon her cycle. In Balkan lore Venus was known as St Venere, and she is still honoured as a patron of marriage by young girls who use her name when wishing for a 'good husband'!

There is a rhyme still used today which was originally addressed to Venus as the Evening Star:

> Star light,
> Start bright,
> First star I see tonight,
> I wish I may,
> I wish I might,
> Have the wish I wish tonight.

Every Zodiac sign has its own particular colour or colours and pinks and blues are associated with Taurus. In addition, green is associated with the planet Venus.

Your planetary symbol is the Bull which in mythology has a fascinating history. Almost every ancient God incarnated at one time or another as a bull, including Minos, the Moon King of the Cretans; Yama, the Hindu Lord of Death who wore a bull's head and was the judge of the underworld; and Shiva, who was Nandi the white bull. The Egyptian Osiris was also worshipped as a bull who was slain annually to atone for the sins of the realm and reincarnated as the Golden Calf. In medieval England, Twelfth Night games contained some remnants of bull worship involving sacrifice, and the sacrificial bull was supposed to have prophetic powers.

As a Taurean, it is often said that when you lose your temper you can be like the proverbial 'bull in a china shop', and that you can be 'bull-headed' when you are in one of your stubborn or obstinate moods. And sometimes when you dig your heels into the ground your stance can also resemble that of a bull! But you don't have to be one of those 'sacrificial bulls', and with Venus, Goddess of Love, as your ruler and the Bull as your symbol you possess romance, refinement, sensuality *and* strength – although not necessarily in equal amounts. By learning more about the Inner You, you will achieve greater balance. Becoming less stubborn and more yielding will add to the impact you make on other people while making you feel better about yourself. And you will continue to rejoice in the love of beauty and artistic pursuits which Venus instills in you and which brings light into even the most difficult days.

THE INNER CHALLENGE – THE OUTER CHANGE

There are bound to be certain areas of your life which don't always work out exactly as you would wish. But the trouble with being a typical Taurus is that you can be far too inclined to bury your head in the sand and go on in the same old way. Where Aries thrives on challenges, you want to be left in peace. However, the marvellous thing about learning more about your Inner Self in relation to your sign is that you will also learn how to find greater fulfilment in all the areas of your life, and start to attain more of your Outer Self's desires too. And it doesn't have to be a sudden 180 degree change – it can be gradual!

RELATIONSHIPS

In love, you are often as stubborn emotionally as you are in every other area of your life! Being sensual, sensuous, sentimental and lovable simply isn't enough, because at the same time you can be too slow at letting someone know how you feel about them. Even though there is often lots of sizzling passion lurking below the surface of most Taureans, and a fair amount of jealousy too, you can sometimes miss out on the chance of a wonderful relationship because you hide your feelings just too long.

It might seem strange to accuse you, whose feet appear to be so very firmly on the ground, of being insecure when it comes to

---

The Outer You   is excited but scared by fiery Aries; dares not admit to being bored by Taurus; cannot keep up with Gemini's chit chat; loves Cancer's sentimental domesticity; dislikes to be bossed by Leo; appreciates Virgo's practical ways; adores the charm and affection of Libra; secretly fantasises about Scorpio; doesn't go for those free and easy Sagittarian ways; is delighted that Capricorn is so, so practical; is not too sure about all that unconventional Aquarian behaviour; tries to tell Pisces that romantic dreams aren't enough for the real world.

The Inner You   empathises with Aries' hidden vulnerability; understands why Taurus *is* Taurus; realises that mental stimulation for Gemini is a big plus; appreciates even more the sensitivity of a warm-hearted Cancer; enjoys making Leo feel proud and happy; understands why Virgo often needs to criticise; remembers never to be too stubborn with easy-going Libra; is fascinated by the attraction of opposites with Scorpio; knows just how to make Sagittarius remain feeling inwardly free; knows how to make materialistic Capricorn appreciate the more sensual side of life; learns that unconventionality can be a whole lot of fun with Aquarius as teacher; finds that those Piscean dreams *can* become reality with just a little help!

love. But when you become more in touch with your Inner Self you will be more aware of the need to create the right balance in your relationships. Of course security will be just as important, but you will understand that to achieve the sort of calm, committed, long-lasting relationships your inner being yearns for you must also be prepared to let go when something *isn't* right.

By delving deeper into your inner being you will find greater self-confidence, and there will be far less conflict between the material needs of the Outer You and the more spiritual yearnings of the Inner You. You will also be inspired to learn more about the inner feelings of all the people who figure in your life so that every relationship becomes more rewarding.

CAREERS AND BUSINESS

Both male and female Taureans often possess creativity in abundance, but you lack the necessary motivation to turn you into stars! However, Barbra Streisand and Jack Nicholson are both movie stars who certainly had the talent plus all the necessary determination and motivation to get to the top, while Shirley MacLaine understood the need to look within and communicate with her Inner Self in order to become even more successful.

Even though you may not want to be a star, you have to admit that deep down you often want the success which stardom brings and that you need a goal to work towards, for which you will willingly put in long hours. But sometimes you lag behind and are too content to take second place – something you cannot afford to do in these times of economic instability when so many people's jobs are at stake.

It's great to be someone who can overcome obstacles and who never worries how much work is involved in achieving your objectives. But by communicating more with the Inner You, you will be able to accomplish even more by not allowing inner frustration or insecurity to develop into a craving for power which brings out a ruthless streak. You will rid yourself of inhibitions which often have you admiring yet fearing the get-up-and-go attitudes of Fire signs like Aries and Leo, and will benefit from being patient at the right moments yet rising to the occasion when a split second decision is called for.

You seem to adhere to discipline so easily in your outer life, and now you can apply a different kind of discipline to allow your inner voice to come through. That voice will help to convince you that by being more spontaneous in your actions, and less pre-occupied with your material status alone, the work put into your chosen career will delight you even more.

You will also begin to realise the importance of feeling happy and fulfilled in your chosen career. It's not that you will suddenly feel the urge to switch careers. Occupations which tend to relate to Taureans, such as banking, accountancy, property dealing, being an economist, estate agent, farmer or architect, will still go hand in hand with the world of the arts. But there will be something new – a recognition that ambition doesn't have to be a dirty word. If you have talent, don't be shy about showing it to the world and start to enjoy the fruits of your labours!

How Do You Handle Decisions?

There is usually no way we can get by without making decisions in our lives, regardless of our star sign. But if you're a fairly typical Taurean you have to face up to the fact that you're sometimes too concerned about making the right decision in a material sort of way, without thinking about whether it's really good for your soul.

You must remember that decision making doesn't have to mean digging your heels stubbornly into the earth and commit-ting yourself to a course of action without taking anyone else's thoughts and ideas into account. And stop hanging on to the past! So often you cling to certain ideas and ideals even when they are outmoded and outworn. Even if you have been burnt once before, it doesn't mean that every single decision you make has to be influenced by that.

No matter what you have to decide upon, if you're prepared to communicate with the still, silent voice within a little more regularly you won't find yourself with such a heavy load to carry when it *is* decision time.

Of course, material issues will continue to be highly important, especially in the 1990s with their continuing tales of economic woe. But your decisions will relate to what is best for you and those closest to you in *every* possible way.

How Do You Handle Conflicts?

Needless to say, once your attitude to decision making begins to change you will also be able to deal with conflicts in a far more relaxed way too.

Your usual attitude often means you tend to hammer things home in a stubborn and selfish way. You refuse to let go on your point of view, and Taurus the Bull can turn into a real bully. But you soon become defensive if somebody has a real go at *you*, so it's about time you were more sensitive to other people's feelings when you're hammering home one of your points!

Often possessed with quite a power complex yourself, it's as though, in your mind, winning a conflict equates with greater power. You can be infuriated by those of us who tend to drift through life caring more about spirituality than material gains, but creating a conflict because of this can be an awful waste of energy.

You often have to cope with feelings of jealousy and resentment, not to mention the usual anger which stems from a conflict with someone you think is being maddeningly inefficient. Think about your opposite sign of Scorpio, so often maligned for being unforgiving and holding on to past slights for ever more, and remember that our opposite sign often makes us look at something we need to know about ourselves, rather like a mirror image! Resolve that you will learn to let go of your negative thoughts if and when conflicts arise in your life.

By going deeper within, and utilising the benefits of techniques such as meditation, you will start to learn that giving way isn't always a sign of weakness but can be a sign of growth in your own personality. Often what seems such a big issue on the surface is really just a test of your inner strength. By becoming more flexible in your arguments, you will discover greater freedom too. You won't have to hang on to the past so much, and you will overcome your fear of feeling in any way inferior which has often been the reason you've stubbornly hung on in conflicts.

You As A Parent

The influence of your ruler Venus means that you will be a kind and loving parent, and your tactile nature means that there will be lots of genuinely affectionate gestures towards your children.

Known as 'the builder' of the Zodiac, you will enjoy building a home for your family, in both the material and the metaphorical sense, and as you become more in tune with your inner voice you will find that you develop more of a carefree and relaxed attitude towards those little rules and regulations you seem to carry in your head!

Don't think of family life as routine – it can be a whole lot of fun too, which is all the more reason not to be as stubborn and inflexible with your offspring as you are with yourself, and indeed with lots of other people too. Remember that while you teach your children the importance of some material security, it's equally important to teach them that it is not the only thing in life. Let them know that they can always talk to you about difficult issues, that you're not so busy beavering away that you don't have time to stop. The importance of good family ties can never be over-stressed, especially in these times when we see so many homeless young people on the streets, an easy prey to abuse and exploitation.

Coping With Life After
Break-Ups Or Bereavements

In some ways it can be harder for you than for other signs to cope with either of these issues. You don't find it easy to accept changes of any kind, especially if they are forced upon you.

You also have a tendency to hold back your deepest feelings, wanting to show yourself as a brave survivor at all costs when any kind of tragedy hits you. But you can also behave childishly, almost stamping your feet on the ground if a relationship ends not by your own choice. You are indeed one of the strongest survivors in the whole Zodiac, but by confiding your deepest feelings to your Inner Self through the meditation technique which you will find on pages 35–6 your almost limitless outer strength will be balanced by the inner strength you gain once you have accepted that change can also be growth. And growth can bring you happiness even during the darkest times.

LIFESTYLE, HEALTH AND DIET

The Taurus lifestyle should be very easy to define, with 'easy' being the operative word. You are not always the most energetic of folk – and in some instances this could be an understatement! Your favourite exercise might well consist of lounging around in a sauna or a jacuzzi, or having a wonderful massage. An easy-going lifestyle is what you dream of, and with your love of the very earth itself you often prefer to live outside large cities and have a garden where you can indulge your love of flowers and plants to your heart's content. You may already be aware that Taureans are renowned for their 'green fingers'.

There is also a sybaritic side to your personality. Taurus is associated with all the senses, and your taste-buds in particular are highly attuned, which means that you can be a true gourmet over food. Just make sure that this doesn't mean your Taurean flesh becomes a little flabby, or you'll need some strenuous form of exercise to balance it! You don't have to turn into a long-distance runner overnight, but don't ever become a 'couch potato' sitting in front of the TV night after night!

Like mind, body and spirit, your lifestyle, health and diet are all intertwined, and it will help you to choose a personal affirmation which you can say to yourself each morning as you get ready for the day. Devise some special words which will be easy for you to follow, or use those that you will find at the end of this chapter. Don't make the excuse that you are so settled into a comfortable routine that there is simply no way you will have time for anything else. That is simply another example of your stubbornness, and if you allow it to predominate you will lose out on a wonderful opportunity to enjoy a more pleasurable lifestyle in which every part of you is in perfect balance.

Since so many of you are extremely fond of listening to music and enjoy many other aspects of the arts, make sure that you're not one of those Taureans who lazily make notes of everything which is showing in town while lounging in an easy chair, and then fail to make the necessary effort to go to the various exhibitions, theatres or concert halls.

Often you are possessed of great creativity yourself, so try to have your lifestyle contain moments when this creativity can be used. Many of you enjoy working in clay, making beautiful ceramics, or trying your hand at sculptured forms. You may also enjoy learning about crystals, or taking up a reflexology class. And since textiles and fabrics are important to you, you might even decide to learn how to make your own clothes, especially as the cost of living continues to rise.

A healthy lifestyle means that you cannot afford to be too 'over the top' in your everyday diet. Rich food once in a while is not going to create havoc, but every day. . . !

Astrologically, Taurus rules the throat and the neck. Sometimes you have problems with your thyroid gland, and it has been surmised that those problems can even arise because mentally you are holding back your deepest thoughts and not expressing the love and creative energy you have within you. All the more reason to be in touch with your Inner Self and allow that same love and creative energy to flow outwards in a positive way.

In developing a more positive lifestyle, you will soon feel the inner benefits and see the outer ones. Your body will respond to your kindness in not over-indulging it with rich foods by looking *and* feeling better. Those of you who are already keen on gardening will enjoy even more the pleasure of eating those vegetables which you have grown with your own hands; and the idea of going for a long brisk walk won't seem such an horrendous thought that you groan out loud! Even if you've been accused of being lazy for years, you will suddenly find yourself raring to go – and anyone who has ever accused you of having a boring lifestyle will have to eat their words.

One word of warning. If you have failed to watch your diet for a long, long time, don't suddenly go on a drastic diet thinking this will start you off on the right track. This is one area where those Taurean traits of patience and perseverance will be the best formula for you, combined with a really well balanced eating regime, and advice from your doctor if necessary.

GROWING OLD GRACEFULLY

Growing old gracefully for you really will depend yet again on your ability to let go of old routines and habits, to accept your new status, to feel proud of your age and what you have achieved so far in your life, and to open up your mind even more. You are fortunate in possessing patience, for if things start to take longer to get done, or need to be overlooked, you will reflect with happiness on what you *have* achieved in your life and not become frustrated about those things which may no longer be possible.

However, no matter how in tune you have become with your Inner Self, you may still have your little moments of concern about your security. As you grow older it is important for you to know that you are handling material issues in the best way possible. You don't want to suddenly develop an extravagant streak!

The wonderful thing is that the security you have developed within will be a blessing that is worth millions and will stand you in good stead for the rest of your life. Growing old gracefully is a time for you to relax and enjoy the rest of your days.

HOW TO GET IN TOUCH WITH THE INNER YOU

At the beginning of this book, I suggested that one way to understand your Inner Self more is to think of it as a little child. As a Taurus, you can easily give that little child a hard time when you're in one of your especially stubborn and inflexible moods.

This is why your own particular form of meditation can be so helpful for you as it will help you to let go and flow more easily with life. You will soon start to feel the inner strength and sense of purpose which will enable you to make any necessary changes.

The Taurus Meditation

Choose a quiet place so that no one can disturb you. Sit comfortably on the floor in a cross legged position (or on a chair if this feels better for you), close your eyes, relax and imagine you are listening to a favourite piece of New Age music playing in the background. Visualise yourself slowly rising above the ground on a cloud, your body feeling weightless because one by one you see any fears or frustrations floating away. Allow your mind to be still, although don't worry if thoughts do start to come in because they will just slide past effortlessly. As you float through the sky you see below you the most beautiful shades of green and all the other colours of Nature. The Earth looks so wonderful from above, and you feel its strength and energy revitalising your own body as you sink into a meditative state for around twenty minutes. At the end of this time allow yourself to drift slowly, slowly down again, feeling its life-force pouring into you as you touch the ground.

Try to do this meditation, or one of your own choice, for twenty minutes a day. And don't worry, you will soon know instinctively when twenty minutes are up.

Of course, you may already have your own way of meditating. That's fine. The important thing is that you recognise the benefits which meditation can bring.

Then, each morning, when you are washing and brushing your teeth, look at yourself in the mirror and affirm to yourself with feeling and conviction:

My inner strength and confidence
help me to move on in life without fear

The more you understand your Inner Self, the easier it will be for you to realise that you don't have to be quite so stubborn and inflexible and quite so rooted to the ground. You will learn that discovering new facets of life can be an adventure you will enjoy!

YOUR PERSONAL GUIDE TO THE FUTURE

By taking note of the advice given in this chapter, you will understand and know yourself much better. Once you do that you will be able to have even more fulfilling relationships in your emotional and your working life. It is not that you will suddenly become a different person, or decide to roam the world without having a permanent home. But your attitude to your life and the way you live it will change. You won't hang on to the dead wood in your life and you'll be flying higher instead of standing so firmly on the ground.

You won't dig your heels in and refuse to budge quite so often on a subject under discussion, or be quite so content to take second place at work when inwardly you're yearning to be more of a star. You will admit that, just like your opposite sign of Scorpio, you can be exceedingly jealous if you fear that the love of your life is flirting a little too much with somebody else – but your newfound inner security will allow you to put everything in its right perspective, and to understand the inner workings of every other star sign too.

Since you can be as dedicated to 'service' as any Virgoan, you may well decide to put your organising talents to good use, perhaps helping those less fortunate than you. You're a positive powerhouse of energy when you want to be and your help will never go unappreciated.

You will have discovered that 'being grounded' doesn't have to mean just standing with your feet firmly on the ground – for when you're in tune with your inner voice it can also mean that you're perfectly balanced in mind, body and soul.

Positive Outlooks	**Possible Pitfalls**
★ Achieving your objectives	★ Liking second place too much!
★ Developing greater creativity	★ Being undecided on your direction
★ Having more self-confidence	★ Holding on to and/or living in the past
★ Enjoying more loving relationships	★ Remaining stuck in a wrong relationship
★ Having a greater spirit of adventure	★ Refusing to take any risks
★ Looking forward to the future	★ Stubbornly clinging to set patterns
★ Becoming less materialistic	★ Putting material issues first

For the typical Taurus, the idea of change in any form could seem daunting at first. But when you get to know and understand your Inner You, you will have no need to fear. The change will be gradual and subtle and your special voyage of self-discovery will be calm and smooth. Don't let it pass you by, and your future can be wonderful!

Gemini

———— ☆ ————

MAY 21 – JUNE 20

Gemini is the third sign of the Zodiac. You are a Masculine, Mutable, Positive sign, and the first of the Air signs. Mercury, Messenger of the Gods, is your planetary ruler, and your planetary symbol is the Twins.

You have a fantastic ability to communicate on almost every level and could easily talk from morning to night with hardly a break! You have masses of charm, you crave excitement and you possess a curiosity about life which never dies, so you are always searching for something new.

Intelligent and very often intellectual, you love knowledge: mental stimulation is the name of the game for you. You're a wonderful asset at dinner parties since you have the ability to mix well with all levels of society. Fun-loving and frolicsome, it's almost impossible for anyone to be bored when they are with a typical Gemini. But, needless to say, because your 'sign of the Twins' gives you a certain duality in your personality you sometimes have the tendency to be almost as impatient as Aries, or as changeable in your decisions as an indecisive Libra. You can also wear yourself out with too much activity for your body *and* your mind.

Obviously, in any astrology book one can only generalise, and perhaps your own particular horoscope contains so many dif-

ferent planetary aspects that your Gemini personality is overshadowed and it would be difficult to guess you were a Gemini.
But that is pure speculation, and meanwhile it's all too easy for
you to be branded with such descriptions as 'two faced and
schizophrenic', or 'overly fickle and flirtatious', and to be accused
of a nervous restlessness which makes it impossible to relax when
you're on the prowl!

Because the brain, nervous system and power of speech all
relate to Gemini, as do your hands, it's not surprising that you
tend to wave your hands and arms about when you're trying to
put a point across to someone else. Nor is it surprising that your
inability to calm your Gemini mind can lead to so many Gemini
insomniacs.

All your thoughts and ideas will be constantly stimulated by the
events taking place in the world in this last decade of the century.
And since you are such a brilliant communicator you will have no
shortage of conversation about them either. The positive side of
this communication cannot be over-estimated, although you're
not necessarily a good listener yourself unless you are totally
fascinated by what you hear. Your tolerance level when it comes
to boredom is usually very, very low. But to be really positive, you
must be prepared to let other people have their say too *and* to
listen to them.

Once you start to take more of an interest in the inner workings
of your psyche, you will begin to understand the importance of
your heart in your everyday life. Mental communication is a
marvellous asset, but 'heartfelt mental communication' is even
more worthwhile.

It's fascinating to me that while you are one of the most
'curious' signs of the Zodiac, that curiosity doesn't always extend
to the inner workings of your own mind, although it is that same
mind which keeps you eternally alert and active and provides you
with your very own elixir of life.

We all have an outer personality and an inner one. Your Outer
You is all chat, chat and more chat, and this sometimes means that
there are occasions when your personality appears to be very
superficial. But getting in touch with the Inner You will help you
to understand not only *who* you are but also *why* you are the *way*
you are. Those three Ws can be a wonderful guide to your future

happiness. So don't nervously wave your hands in the air and say that you don't have the time or the inclination to be curious, because it simply isn't true! Think about your inner personality rather like a little child, and don't be surprised to find that your little Gemini child will really enjoy discovering more about itself if it will only sit down long enough to begin.

It's wonderful to be a Gemini with your insatiable curiosity, so be inspired to experiment a little – even if it is somewhat warily at first – and discover the hidden facets of your Inner You. Perhaps the first thing you will have to do is to admit that there are times when it is more worthwhile to be the listener than the speaker; for you will learn nothing from your inner voice unless you can first train your mind to be still. Further on in this chapter you will discover a meditation and affirmation especially for you, which will help you to do just that.

Creating the right balance between your outer and inner personality isn't something which happens overnight. It's something which, sadly, Geminis like Marilyn Monroe and Judy Garland never did manage to achieve. But as a Gemini you have so many positive aspects, including excellent powers of reason and an abundance of versatility, that it won't be *that* difficult! Besides, apart from your talent for communication you have a thirst for knowledge which is almost as great as that of your opposite sign of Sagittarius – you simply have to concentrate more deeply on what lies below the surface and learn something about expressing your real feelings.

Of course it is wonderful to be someone who is invariably interested in everything going on around you. But the 'grass on the other side' isn't *always* greener, and what is going on deep inside you can be just as stimulating as some of that glib cocktail party chat which might figure all too often in your life.

Start to think of Mercury, Winged Messenger of the Gods, as being your very own messenger with a special message to impart, a message which will help you to live your own life not only in a happier and more relaxed way, but in a way which will also bring more people into your life who are true friends, and not simply more of the myriad acquaintances who can be attracted to you rather like moths to a flame, but with whom you sometimes discover you have too little in common.

Sometimes it's almost as though there is something within you which doesn't want to grow up and accept responsibility for your actions. But you can't remain Peter Pan all your life! Mind, body and soul – they all go together, yet while you are an expert in speaking your mind you can be something of a coward when it comes to letting your soul have its say. Now it's time to let your inner voice give you that inner security we all need – even you!

Positive and Negative, Yin and Yang, we need them all, and once you start to feel the balance between that Outer and Inner You, your life in the 1990s will become even more stimulating.

Pathways To Success In The 1990s

★ Stop skating on the surface of life, and get to understand more about what's happening within.

★ Stay a scintillating conversationalist, but resolve to be a fascinated listener too.

★ Take time off to rest that helter-skelter mind if you want to gain some inner knowledge about life.

★ Always remember to listen to what your heart is saying if you want to reach the Inner You.

★ Prove you can be capable and responsible as well as socially charismatic.

★ Think of each day as a new learning experience – and enjoy it.

Your Ruling Planet . . . Mercury, Winged Messenger of the Gods

One of the major influences on a male or female Gemini is your planetary ruler. Mercury, the ruler of Gemini, is the planet representing communication, speech and commerce and was known in mythology as the Winged Messenger of the Gods. So it's no wonder that you are such an avid messenger and teller of tales. Astrologically, Mercury is the fastest moving of all the planets – producing that mental and nervous energy which is so typical of you. You can thank Mercury for your intellectual prowess, your ability to switch ideas at the drop of a hat, and your power to communicate with the world at large.

Although the Romans called him Mercury, the Greeks named him Hermes – the God of magic, letters, medicine and occult wisdom. He was considered to be even older than Greece itself and was the original 'hermaphrodite', united with Aphrodite in one body.

In the body Mercury relates to the brain and to the respiratory and nervous systems. Because of this link with the nervous system it is said that the B Complex vitamins are related to Mercury.

Every sign has its own particular colour or colours, and there are a few especially associated with Gemini. Yellow, navy blue and grey are often favourites.

It is usually said that the planetary symbol for Gemini, the sign of the Twins, relates to Castor and Pollux, the twin Roman Gods of the morning and evening star. And in mythology there were many sets of twins, all relating to light and darkness – hence the duality of the Gemini personality in astrology, and perhaps one of the main reasons for people sometimes accusing you of being something of a Dr Jekyll and Mr Hyde. However, blaming Castor and Pollux for your changeability is simply not on! The Gemini planetary symbol is made of two upright lines in between two horizontal ones, to represent doorposts and lintel. The Gemini twins of ancient times were supposed to be the guardians of all doors and entrances, and were especially identified with the sacred pillars of Jachin and Boaz at Jerusalem.

Throughout the ages there have been many famous Gemini writers, including Thomas Mann, Jean Paul Sartre, Walt Whitman, Conan Doyle, Thomas Hardy, Saul Bellow, Françoise Sagan, Margaret Drabble, Athol Fugard and David Hare. That great thinker, Bertrand Russell was also a Gemini.

With Mercury, planet of communication, as your ruler, and the Twins as your planetary symbol, you are sure to be a fascinating person in many many ways. In learning more about the Inner You, you have a worthwhile and interesting challenge – developing a calmness born from inner knowledge which can go hand in hand with your agile and adaptable mind. This will allow you to harness your energy so that you can see what lies below the surface of life in these ever-changing times; for then you can perhaps do something truly worthwhile with your skills of communication.

THE INNER CHALLENGE – THE OUTER CHANGE

There are sure to be some areas of your life which don't always turn out exactly as you would like, if you are truthful enough to admit it! If you're a typical Gemini, you are so used to mentally detaching yourself from anything which seems the slightest bit dull that you can often go along for a long time without ever scratching the surface of what you're really feeling.

The following areas will all be important to you in one way or another. If your natural curiosity will now prompt you to get a little closer to the still, silent voice within, it will be well rewarded.

RELATIONSHIPS

In love, it takes someone very special to get to know your inner personality. It's not that you're shy – far from it. But it's so hard to get you to stop thinking! Your mercurial mind never seems to stand still for a moment, and you seem so intent on receiving your 'fix' of mental stimulation that you not only refuse to look within, but often behave thoughtlessly towards people you really do love deeply.

Deep down, you would usually admit that you long for the perfect partner – that special soulmate who will love, cherish and admire you. Flirtatious you may be, but when you *do* meet the right person you don't necessarily want to be fickle. So if you're going to start listening to your inner voice, remember to *take* some of its advice too!

One of the things which will happen when you delve deeper into your Inner Self is that you will recognise and accept what you truly yearn for in a relationship. Learning about and appreciating your own inner feelings will in turn create a positive step towards learning more about the inner feelings of everyone who is a part of your life.

The Outer You sees Aries as just a quick flirtation; finds Taurus a good listener, but sometimes dull; simply *has* to appreciate another Gemini, at least on the surface; worries that Cancer might hem you in; falls headlong for flamboyant Leo; ends up arguing with pernickety Virgo; fears that Libra wants permanence too soon; senses mental *and* sexual stimulation with Scorpio; is annoyed that Sagittarius just might know more than you; is often too social for a really staid Capricorn; is not quite sure about all that Aquarian unpredictability; thinks Pisces is just too dreamy for words.

The Inner You takes sufficient time to appreciate the challenge of Aries; enjoys discovering sensuous feelings with Taurus; learns a lot from the mirror image of another Gemini; stops flitting around and appreciates cosy domesticity with Cancer; is willing to concede that Leo really is a star; appreciates that Virgo only wants the best for you; loves the calming influence of peaceful Libra; realises that talk never will be enough with Scorpio; recognises that intellectual equality can be found with Sagittarius; understands that Capricorn needs to be helped to feel secure; plays beautiful music with freedom-loving Aquarius; realises that an idle flirtation cannot take the place of true romantic love when Pisces comes along.

CAREERS AND BUSINESS

Both male and female Geminians are wonderfully versatile and amazingly innovative when it comes to career and business issues. However, at the same time your attention span is limited, your concentration can go from variable to negligible, and your boredom threshold is rarely something to write home about.

You're often a veritable jack-of-all-trades, brimming over with talent but sometimes lacking the discipline necessary to carry any one task through to the end. The idea of being successful is interesting to you, but making a financial fortune tends to seem less important than feeling free. The thought of a strict regime and routine is horrendous to most people born under your sign, as too is anything which appears to be mindless in any shape or form. Your inborn restlessness combined with your seeming lack of ambition can mean that even when you are working in something you really enjoy you still lack direction. The curiosity inherent in your mercurial mind is always tempting you to look for something more exciting. Sometimes you hold yourself back in your professional life by again giving in to that 'grass is always greener on the other side' belief.

Without any doubt, as a Gemini you're a 'people' person, and naturally enough it's the way you communicate that will be your biggest asset in everything related to career and business. There is often something flamboyant and extrovert in the way you work – Prince, Jason Donovan, Sandra Bernhard, Boy George and Joan Collins are all Gemini, as too are Barry Manilow and Steffi Graf. And you can be pretty convincing when putting your message across – as Hedda Hopper, Mary Whitehouse and Robert Maxwell have all demonstrated!

By learning to communicate with your inner voice, and finding your own personal way to still your ever active mind, you will discover that your ruling planet Mercury is one of the greatest bonuses you could wish for. If your mind is trained from within, its potential on the outside is phenomenal, and later in this chapter you will find the meditation and affirmation which will help you to do this. Mind, body and soul – they need to harmonise together in order to get the best out of your star sign. Start off by utilising the power of Mercury and it won't be long before you will begin to find an inner balance which gives a whole new positive vibration to your career and business life.

Don't worry, you won't suddenly gravitate to a dull and boring job. Your goal will always be to involve yourself in something interesting, and Gemini careers such as journalism, TV, radio, computers, publishing, sales, teaching, politics, travel, all forms of writing and anything which involves languages will always appeal. And they will become even more exciting and fulfilling, when you concentrate on them more!

How Do You Handle Decisions?

For someone who is so adept at using your versatile mind, it's almost extraordinary to discover that you have the most amazing way of procrastinating. You truly can be almost as indecisive as Libra over the simplest of decisions! The reason for this is often very simple. It all relates to your fear of showing what you really feel below the surface.

Once you learn the value of listening to your inner voice you will be amazed how much easier it will be to evaluate all the pros and cons of situations and come to the right decision. No longer will you confuse yourself by acting how you *think* you should act without listening to your true feelings! Once you really do start to go inside yourself and let your mind learn how to become still you will start to see everything in a different way and decision making will take on a whole new positive light.

You often need to talk things over with other people rather than trust your own intuition, but once you start to silently communicate with your inner being the need for this will lessen. And you will become a much stronger person too.

How Do You Handle Conflicts?

Once your attitude to decision making starts to alter, conflicts will also become easier to handle.

Meanwhile, you will probably have to admit that the way you tackle conflicts generally means you will go on the attack, censuring your opponent almost as much as if you were a critical and analytical Virgo! It almost seems impossible for you to imagine that you could be wrong about something. But the truth is so often that you have simply refused to go deep inside yourself to question whether you might possibly be at fault – let alone listen to what your opponent has to say for more than a few seconds.

The duality of the sign of the Twins enables you to give yourself a mask: the side of you which might feel guilty is hidden below the surface. Your Gemini mind enables you to come up with all the answers, which are very convincing – while your Gemini emotions, which could tell you that the biggest conflict of all is with yourself, are locked away.

This is where the benefit of listening to that inner voice is so immense that you can no longer afford to ignore it. Reflect on your opposite sign of Sagittarius – the truth seeker, the sage and counsellor of the Zodiac, the sign of the higher mind. Sagittarius is always prepared to search far and wide for the truth, and you can do the same since there is always something of our opposite star sign inside ourselves.

Always try to utilise your powers of communication for the best on all possible levels. Conflicts only make you nervous and jumpy, and learning how to handle them in these simple ways will make your nervous system grateful for ever more! In the meantime, don't involve yourself unnecessarily with people who irritate you by being uninterested in what goes on around them, for you're bound to be worlds apart.

YOU AS A PARENT

In many ways you could be the perfect parent – someone with your Peter Pan quality, interested in so many diverse things, eternally young at heart and full of fun, and encouraging your children to read and write and look at life from an early age. That's on the plus side. But the negative side of all this of course might easily be that you sometimes don't allow enough time for your children. And what can be worse is that you don't listen properly to their real needs.

The wonderful part about getting in touch with your own emotions is that you will truly understand how important it is to communicate with your offspring on every level, so that communication between you will always be deep and fulfilling. One of the greatest benefits of this will be that your children will know that they can always talk to you about anything, and that you will truly share their happiness and sorrows. You will understand their deepest feelings, hopes and aspirations, so that you can always give them the advice and support they need as they grow up in a world where it can be harder than ever to remain positive.

COPING WITH LIFE AFTER BREAK-UPS OR BEREAVEMENTS

In this kind of situation it is usually so much better once you have admitted to yourself, and indeed everyone else, that you *do* have deep feelings, and when you let them come to the surface rather than bottling them all up so that your nervous system has to work like crazy to stay in balance! This is especially important as Gemini rules the nervous system, and you don't want to increase the risk of unnecessary stress and tension in your mind, body or your soul.

Naturally, coping with break-ups or bereavements is not easy for anyone, but allowing your inner voice to teach you how to calm your mind and release your fears and anxieties will be a wonderful benefit. The meditation and affirmation on pages 52–3 will also be a great help. Remember that with Mercury, planet of the mind, ruling your sign, it really is your mental attitude that affects your life most strongly. This is definitely one instance when you can count your blessings to know that you're someone who will always find new and positive interests to occupy your mind.

LIFESTYLE, HEALTH AND DIET

The Gemini lifestyle can be as changeable as your moods, but invariably the constant factor is that variety is the spice of your life. However, since you're always on the go, indulging yourself with everything that stimulates your mind, you often exhaust yourself completely.

This is the right moment to remind you again that, since the nervous system is ruled by your sign, the importance of creating the right balance in mind, body and soul is extremely important for you.

You don't have to completely alter your lifestyle, but once you have learnt to appreciate the value of those quiet moments when your mind starts to unwind and your body can relax you will also begin to achieve a wonderful inner peace and calm which in time will definitely enhance your enjoyment of life. The thought of meditation of any kind may seem very difficult to the typical Gemini, but it really is worth the effort (there is more on this later in this chapter).

Entertainment is vital in your lifestyle, and almost every Gemini I have known makes every effort to keep up with the latest plays, films and books. Your thirst for knowledge and your dislike of missing anything which sounds worthwhile make you a veritable mine of information for the rest of the Zodiac. And it's never too late for you to take up a new interest. I know one Gemini lady of seventy-four who has to spend a great deal of time looking after her husband who has Alzheimer's Disease, but has still managed to join a Music Appreciation class.

Yoga is wonderful for you, for it is said that its teachings link the human mind to a lake with rising and falling waves, and that Yoga itself neutralises the waves of feeling and restless consciousness – so much a part of Gemini. And some of you may enjoy Biofeedback, Stress Management or Relaxation Training to help you relax in a way which appeals to that Gemini intellect. But you can be inordinately lazy when it comes to any form of sport. As far as you're concerned, it's invigorating to watch Wimbledon on the TV but as for stepping on a tennis court yourself . . . that's something else! However, something like T'ai Chi or the Alexander Technique could be wonderfully therapeutic for you.

Your lifestyle, health and diet are very much linked together, so remember that it's very important not to spend so much time rushing around in circles that your health and diet start to suffer. And it's important for you to get the right amount of sleep. I've noticed that Gemini people can stay up all hours of the night having wonderful conversations, arguing their points with brilliance, or watching highly controversial programmes or movies on late night TV, but when it comes to an important appointment first thing in the morning there is a dullness in those normally sparkling Gemini eyes, and a definite lack of vivacity and vitality. Make sure you eat properly, and try to avoid that strong espresso after dinner so that you avoid insomnia, which is so often a Gemini trait.

The other health problems which can relate to your sign are bronchial infections, neuritis in the arms and shoulders, and nervous debility. Because Gemini rules the lungs you can have problems with breathing and respiratory disease, and this is one important reason for you to balance your outer and inner personalities and stop allowing that ever active mind to control your life and dissipate your energies.

Dissipation of your natural energies is in fact one of your biggest faults, which is a very good reason to begin to plan your lifestyle in a more organised way. More than any other star sign, you need to set a big notepad and pencil in front of you at the start of each day with your agenda written in.

A more positive approach to your lifestyle, acknowledging that your Inner Self really *can* help you understand those inner workings of your mind and calm you during moments when your nervous energy sends you into a flat spin, will in turn make you even more loved by your relatives and friends.

GROWING OLD GRACEFULLY

Growing old gracefully for a typical Gemini, whether male or female, is rarely a difficult feat. That Peter Pan quality, which never completely leaves you, means that your interest in people and places never lessens. You will probably still be an avid reader, keeping up with everything that takes place in the world and probably thinking up ways for you to still do your bit in it.

It wouldn't surprise me if there are many elderly Geminians around who one day decide to sit down and write their memoirs, even if they are only going to be passed down to relatives and close friends.

But for you, growing old gracefully in a perfect way also means accepting who you are for what you are, and finally recognising that you don't have to hide your innermost feelings or simply skim along on the surface of life. You can enjoy yourself so much more by balancing your mind, body *and* soul.

Enjoy your favourite pleasures in life, but enjoy knowing yourself better too!

How To Get In Touch
With The Inner You

At the beginning of this book I suggested that one way to learn more about your Inner Self is to think of it as a little child, and as a Gemini you should maybe think of it as your little Twin! Learn to listen to your twin for it will have valuable information to impart.

In order to do this, your own particular form of meditation can be very helpful as it will help you to still your busy mind and allow you to let go of that continuous stream of thoughts, and to flow with what life has to offer you.

The Gemini Meditation

Sit comfortably on the floor in a cross legged position (or, if this is not comfortable, on a chair), close your eyes and visualise yourself as a beautiful butterfly flitting through the air calmly and contentedly, happy to fly effortlessly with no desire to stop even though all around are exotic and beautiful flowers stretching ever upwards into the sky. Allow your mind to slowly still itself. Don't worry if thoughts insist on coming in – think of them as more butterflies and let them go past, rejoicing in the variety of their different colours. Allow yourself to sink into a state of meditation as gradually your restlessness disappears and your mind becomes ever more calm and still. After about twenty minutes visualise the butterflies gently disappearing from your view.

Try to do this twice a day. You will start to find that your mind really does become less restless and that your concentration on the things which are really important to you will improve so that you can achieve much more in your daily life.

Of course, you may already have your own particular meditation. The important thing is that whichever way you choose to meditate you recognise the benefits it can bring you.

Then each morning, when you wash and brush your teeth, look at yourself in the mirror and affirm to yourself with feeling and conviction:

With a calm mind and open heart
I will exercise control in all things

The more you understand and communicate with your Inner Self, the easier it will be for you to lose your outward restlessness and achieve greater peace, which in turn will lead to increased clarity and perception.

YOUR PERSONAL GUIDE TO THE FUTURE

By following the advice offered in this chapter you will understand and know yourself much better, and then you will be able to have even more fulfilling relationships in your emotional and your working life. You will not suddenly become completely different or lose your desire for mental excitement, but your attitude to life and to your true feelings will be different, and you won't be blocking yourself by thinking just too much. You will have learnt to detach yourself from your own ideas so that you can see all sides of every situation in a calm and balanced way. Your mind won't be at constant battle with your emotions, but it won't send you off on tangents either. You will no longer have to think that the grass could be greener on the other side, for you will have everything you need deep within your own being.

Commitments of any kind will no longer pose a threat to your freedom, for you will have achieved the perfect level of understanding with the people you care for the most. And because you are always so aware of what you see and read you will have a greater understanding of the problems so many people now have to encounter because of job losses, terminal illnesses and broken homes. You may even discover you have hidden talents which can be of immense benefit in one way or another.

Positive Outlooks

★ Being able to understand yourself better
★ Detaching yourself from your mind
★ Gaining emotional and mental balance
★ Seeing all sides of a subject
★ Working out a constant life pattern
★ Keeping your heart and mind open
★ Developing your inner faith
★ Recognising the strength of commitments

Possible Pitfalls

★ Refusing to look within
★ Allowing your mind to play tricks
★ Worrying too much about yourself
★ Blocking anyone else's viewpoint
★ Remaining far too fickle
★ Being unwilling to believe in the power of love
★ Fooling yourself and others
★ Still being a social butterfly

For the typical Gemini, the idea of inner change might seem almost fearful at first. But when you get to know and understand the Inner You it will be as though you have found a light at the end of a tunnel. The clarity of vision and thought you will discover can make your life more enjoyable on a deeper level than you would ever have thought possible. The Twins will be equal partners – at last!

Cancer

☆

JUNE 21 – JULY 21

Cancer is the fourth sign of the Zodiac. You are a Feminine, Cardinal, Negative sign, the first of the Water signs. The Moon is your planetary ruler and your planetary symbol is the Crab.

A warm, loving, friendly, caring, sensitive, sentimental, compassionate human being and the proud possessor of very powerful emotions and an extremely good memory – that's you. People sometimes make jokes about your having a 'moon face', but it's certainly true that you do have extremely expressive faces. Robin Williams is a perfect example.

You are also the home-lover of the Zodiac, and one of the most maternal, paternal, devoted and domesticated signs of all. Looking after the people you care for is like second nature to you and you genuinely enjoy doing it. In the 1990s, when more and more people seem to be going through problems of one sort or another, it's fantastic to be someone who really cares about what is happening in the world. Princess Diana is a good example of a caring mother whose feelings for humanity shine in her face, even during the times when she has been going through immense personal problems herself.

Your typical Cancerian ability to empathise with other people is renowned, as is your sensitivity to atmosphere and ambience. But it is important not to let yourself be too influenced by what others say or do, for although you usually have a good sense of humour you're not too happy if someone else's humour is directed against *you*. At such times it's not for nothing that you are sometimes called 'crabby'. You invariably seem to have built a protective hard shell around you into which you retreat when you feel that your own personal world is threatened in any way, or when one of your famous Cancerian 'moods' descends upon you – which isn't always at Full Moon time as people sometimes think!

Unfortunately, because you *are* possessed with such varying mood-swings, you are often accused of having a hypersensitive personality, a sudden temper, possessive and clinging ways, a propensity to be totally saturated by your own emotions and the ability to worry almost as much as Virgo, which if you're not careful can lead to stomach upsets and even ulcers!

Obviously, in any astrology book one can only generalise, and perhaps your own personal horoscope contains so many diverse planetary aspects that your Cancerian personality is submerged and no one would even know you *are* a Cancerian. But this doesn't happen too often, and it is usually quite easy to pick you out of a crowd.

What *is* true is that you 'feel' everything, almost always with an intensity which can be overwhelming. This can make you very psychic, and indeed you are among the most intuitive and perceptive signs of the Zodiac. So it's about time you had more faith in yourself and started to trust more frequently those very intuitive feelings and psychic flashes which the influence of the Moon, your ruling planet, has bequeathed to you.

Just like your opposite sign of Capricorn, you have a need for material security and possess an inborn ability for self-protection in material issues which will never leave you. There is also a strongly practical side to your nature which often seems to contrast with the romantically dreamy part of your personality.

We all have an outer personality and an inner one. In your case learning to understand the inner one in greater depth can be a real bonus, for you will attain greater inner security and discover more about your deepest feelings in a very positive way. And you will also achieve greater awareness as to your true destiny in life. Soft and sensitive you may be, but there is a strong desire in you to acquire what you need, and a tenacity to hang on at times when adversity might arise, which is also a definite bonus these days. You will find your very own meditation technique and affirmation to help you to understand the Inner You later in this chapter. Meanwhile, you could think of this inner personality rather like a sensitive and vulnerable little child who needs to feel warm and secure and to possess greater initiative.

The Inner You will allow you to create a very special relationship between your inner and outer personalities, bringing about a balance which will help you to recognise that the Cancerian home truly is where the heart is.

It may be a daunting thought to pierce through your protective shell and venture into the depths of your inner being. Perhaps you are scared that you will sink even more into your emotions, and lose yourself in your feelings to such an extent that you will be caught up in a dream-like reverie which becomes an escape from the reality of day to day living. However, when you *are* prepared to delve into your inner personality you will start to discover a new strength of purpose which will enable you to rise above your famous Cancerian moods.

The Moon, your ruler, controls the tides of the sea and its powerful influence is always felt on your emotions. Listen to its message, for it can teach you wisely that you have no need to seek an escape from unhappy moments or situations, but can learn a powerful lesson from each and every day. The Outer Cancerian fears rejection, but your Inner You will teach you to love yourself for who you really are.

As a Water sign, you have an inherent instinct as to the natural flow of life. You know you cannot control everything around you. At the same time you recognise the greater potential within you by allowing your positive energies to flow freely without the burden of unnecessary negative thoughts or actions.

When you truly listen to what your inner voice is telling you, you will never be a frightened little crab who scuttles away from the unknown and hides deep inside that shell, or who holds on to old thought patterns and routines too long.

Your imagination can be a wonderfully positive influence on the one hand; but on the other it can also make you worry unnecessarily about the smallest things. There is also a tendency to indulge in self-pity and to be extremely jealous and possessive when you're in love!

At times you can look too much at the negative side of life instead of the bright side. One way to overcome this is to think about a glass of water filled to the half-way mark. The Negative You will see the glass as half empty – but the Positive You will encourage you to see that same glass as half full. This may seem like a silly exercise, but why not try it? You can easily apply it to any area of your life and it will help you to snap out of moments of feeling sorry for yourself!

Start to open yourself up more to the amazing potential you have within you. Enjoy communicating with your Inner Self – it is one of the most powerful assets you have, and it's all yours. Just like your opposite sign of Capricorn you have a deep-rooted need for security, but don't worry that discovering more about your deepest feelings could make you in some way more vulnerable, for the opposite is true. Listen to your intuition and don't be afraid to take that quantum leap, for you will then discover a new kind of inner peace and security that no one can take away.

Positive and Negative, black and white, Yin and Yang, we have them all. But when you find the right balance between the Outer and the Inner You, you're on the pathway to a more contented and fulfilling life.

PATHWAYS TO SUCCESS IN THE 1990s

★ Use your powerful intuition to help you make the right move at the right time.
★ Always be caring about others, but remember to do what's best for you too – and don't take on *too* many problems.
★ Start to see the humour in life as well as its sad side – it's the best way to live.
★ And resolve to laugh at yourself too – at least sometimes!
★ Develop your inner security so that what goes on outside doesn't hurt too much.
★ Always try to feel happy in your surroundings, both at home and at work – you'll achieve far more that way.

YOUR RULING PLANET . . . The Moon

One of the major influences on a male or female Cancerian is your planetary ruler. Apart from your Cancerian Sun, the Moon is the most important planet in your horoscope, and no matter where it was placed at the moment of your birth it will have a profound effect on your emotions.

The power of the Moon has always been respected and in ancient days it was worshipped by people all over the world, sometimes revered as a God but more often as a Goddess, the feminine force of the Cosmos. As a Goddess the Moon has been called the Great Mother or Mother Earth and has been worshipped as the goddess of abundance and fertility.

If you have read my previous book *Moon Signs for Lovers* you will already know that many names were given to the Moon by different races and in different times. Some of the best known of these are: Artemis, one of the most important Greek divinities and sister of the Sun God; Diana, the Roman equivalent of Artemis; Hecate, a mysterious divinity of the Greeks who was a Moon Goddess and also thought to be a Goddess of the Earth, her great powers were honoured by all the immortal Gods, and because of them she was also identified with Selene or Luna in heaven, Diana or Artemis on Earth, and Persephone or Proserpina in the lower world; Isis, Egyptian wife of Osiris and mother of Horus – originally the Earth Goddess and afterwards the Moon Goddess; Metztli, the Aztec Moon Goddess; Parvati, the Moon Goddess of the Hindus; Shing-Moo, the Chinese Moon Goddess – Queen of the Heavens; Thoth, the Egyptian Moon God of wisdom and learning who was also the inventor of magic; and Ur, an Oriental Moon God and also an Assyrian Fire God.

The Moon is related to birth and motherhood, and to the stomach, breasts, digestive and sympathetic nervous systems, bodily fluids, secretions of the glands and digestive juices, and the mucous membranes. But it is certainly on your emotions and feelings that it has its major effect.

Just as the Moon governs the tides of the sea, so it influences the very soul of your being. While your ego relates to the Sun, the Moon relates to your unconscious state, your emotions, your instincts and your habits. It also relates very much to women: its twenty-eight day cycle corresponds to the menstrual cycle, and a woman's moods during this cycle relate to the Moon's phases. It has a strong relationship to the tides, and it has been said that all the Earth's waters were from the womb of the Moon in the same way that the foetus of an unborn child is protected by the water in a woman's womb.

Every Zodiac sign has its own particular colour or colours, and silver, pale green and smoky colours predominate for you.

Your planetary symbol is the Crab although the ancient Egyptians also portrayed Cancer as a scarab, another creature associated with the moon.

With the Moon as your planetary ruler, your sensitivity, compassion and intuition can help you soar to the heights of emotion and creativity. Its relationship to the Inner You is an amazing bonus – it can help to teach you more about yourself than you may have realised, so use its influence well. By understanding more about your vulnerability and emotional needs you will become stronger and more mature so that you can help others more too.

The Inner Challenge –
The Outer Change

There are bound to be certain areas of your life which don't always turn out exactly as you would like, always supposing of course that you are truthful. If you are a typical Cancer there is often a tendency for you to cling on to people and situations, thus relinquishing your own independence – so the idea of change is something which can send you scurrying into your protective shell or descending into a grey if not black mood. However, sometimes it simply isn't possible for our lives to go in the same old ways any more.

The following areas will be important to you in one way or another, and the beautiful part of learning more about your Inner Self in relation to your sign is that you can learn how to achieve more contentment and fulfilment too.

RELATIONSHIPS

At first it could seem that there is hardly any difference between your outer personality and the Inner You when it comes to love. Your emotional desires and needs seem to stand out in black and white, while your desire to nurture and protect the people you love doesn't go unnoticed by anyone who is involved with you.

But it's the clinging side of your personality which can bring you problems, and you can be as jealous and possessive as any Aries, Taurus or Scorpio can ever be! Sometimes important relationships can falter by the wayside because of your too

---

The Outer You is overwhelmed by impulsive Aries; feels safe but fairly unemotional with Taurus; is slightly threatened by Gemini's flirtatious ways; recognises the mirror image of another Cancer; dislikes being in the limelight which Leo thrives upon; feels insecure when criticised by Virgo; doesn't understand the indecisiveness of Libra; is somewhat frightened by Scorpio's intensity; worries that Sagittarius is just too adventurous; looks for security in Capricorn; finds Aquarius too cool and detached even when in love; fantasises about romantic bliss with Pisces.

The Inner You appreciates the 'child' beneath the somewhat brash exterior of Aries; revels in the sensual *and* sensitive touch of Taurus; discovers the bliss of good communication with Gemini; truly understands the deepest needs of Cancer; recognises why Leo loves to take centre stage; refuses to be intimidated by Virgo's somewhat fussy ways; feels life could be perfect bliss with Libra; learns to understand that even invincible Scorpio's emotions can be bruised at times; delights in seeing the positive side of life with Sagittarius; finds ways to make hard-working Capricorn enjoy even more security in romantic love; appreciates that a little unpredictability in life with Aquarius can be a whole lot of fun; decides that a romantic soulmate like Pisces can brighten the dullest of days.

obvious need for someone special in your life, or because you cling on because of your own personal fears and insecurities or allow your mood swings to control you. So once you realise that the greatest security comes from being at one with yourself – and yes, loving yourself too – you will be able to enjoy each and every relationship without the fear of losing something which is precious to you.

Think of the Inner You as a good friend who can help you balance your emotions in a very positive way, so that self-doubt can soon be a thing of the past no matter what events have taken place in your life.

By delving deeper into your inner being, you will develop greater trust in your instincts and sensitivity, and will be able to recognise with greater ease the difference between the bonding of two partners on a material plane and that of a more spiritual relationship on a true mind, body and soul level. Your mood swings will also diminish as you become more inwardly balanced.

CAREERS AND BUSINESS

As a Cancerian male or female you are often as ambitious as your opposite sign of Capricorn. Those of you who *are* ambitious want to be leaders rather than followers, and your goal is invariably to achieve the maximum material security for yourself and your loved ones. Whether you're a boss or an employee, making money is of prime importance for the typical Cancerian.

However, you are especially susceptible to your working conditions and ambience. In the wrong atmosphere you are rather like a fish out of water, and as a consequence your work can suffer. Working alone is not necessarily what you enjoy most, but amenable and agreeable colleagues are a must for someone who can be so sensitive.

Your ambition to reach the peaks of material security certainly doesn't deteriorate with age – Barbara Cartland is a fantastic example of a Cancerian woman whose energy is eternally unflagging when it comes to writing her books and promoting herself, while David Hockney, Richard Branson, Jennifer Saunders, Sylvester Stallone and Pierre Cardin are also prime examples of Cancerians determined to rise to the top in their chosen fields.

There are those among you who throw yourselves and your emotions into your work wholeheartedly to make up for something lacking in your personal life. Then you take it even more seriously, and can be totally driven in your quest for success in such a materialistic way that you sometimes become hard and embittered, working only for your pay cheque.

By communicating more with your Inner Self you will learn to understand and accept your own particular emotional needs for your working life better. There is nothing worse than to be frustrated in what you are doing. Getting more in touch with your deepest emotions will perhaps also make you realise that material security, while important, doesn't always have to take the place of creative fulfilment and the contentment of working at something you really enjoy. You will learn to use your sensitivity in a more positive way, allowing the power of the Moon to enhance your intuition so that it acts as a guide in your everyday life and enables you to see that your inner security is just as vital – perhaps even more so – as what is going on outside. I'm naturally not disputing that, in these times when the media are full of stories of the hardships the world is facing, material security is not important. I'm just pointing out that there needs to be a balance between hard work for money and creative fulfilment.

You are particularly suited to work which enables you to make full use of your financial abilities and could be a brilliant economist, something powerful in the banking world, or very successful in the hotel or property business. Other good careers for Cancerians are dealing in antiques, teaching, writing, nursing, or veterinary or social work. And because you are so sensitive to the moods of people you may even turn to politics if you feel you can really achieve something worthwhile. But always listen to the still, silent voice within you – no matter which career you choose.

How Do You Handle Decisions?

There will always be decisions of one kind or another to be made in life. The trouble with being a typical Cancer is that you so often retreat into your shell each time one comes along, or scowl and show your discontent at the very thought of having to decide upon something when you're not in the right mood.

Your reasons for this unease at decision making can vary and are not necessarily because you feel uncertain about things. You also often genuinely hate to upset or annoy someone else.

However, by communicating directly with your Inner Self you will find it becomes easier to trust your intuition and to have greater self-confidence. You will realise that what is really important is to have total faith in your beliefs and actions, no matter what has gone on in the past. No longer will you cling to old memories, or remember decisions which backfired upon you. And you will start to see beyond your material desires and expectations which have sometimes also coloured the way you make decisions.

Your emotional feelings invariably influence the way you think when decisions are called for, and when you've been unhappy you have sometimes made your unhappiness an excuse for escaping from making a decision. Your Inner You will enable you to rise above this and you will start to find more happiness too.

How Do You Handle Conflicts?

Once your attitude to decision making begins to alter, conflicts will also be easier to handle. In the meantime you probably have to admit that one of the usual ways for you to handle any form of conflict is to get into one of your 'down' moods, even when you can't blame it on the Full Moon!

Because you are such a sensitive Water sign your emotions can get far too easily out of control, and perhaps you truly think that retreating into your shell yet again really is the best thing to do. We all soon know you hate being laughed at, and that anyone who tells you to throw away old letters, photographs or other memories of your past is going to be told off in no uncertain way. And you may look at askance at the devil-may-care attitude of Aries, Gemini or Aquarius.

By listening to your inner voice, and admitting to yourself that conflicts can so often be avoided by taking a calmer and more disciplined stance to whatever upsets you, you will gain power over your emotions and won't over-react so much.

Another effect of listening to that voice within is that you will sense more than ever when conflicts are likely to arise, so that you will be able to avoid them more often.

Conflicts can have such a negative effect not only on your emotions but also on your health. Cancer rules the stomach and alimentary canal which means that you can be prone to nervous stomachs and upsets in your digestive system and even risk getting ulcers when upset. So think how wonderful it will be to discover how to avoid upsets in the first place!

YOU AS A PARENT

Because you have such strong maternal or paternal instincts you can be one of the best parents in the whole Zodiac. It's certainly true that you usually love to have children around you and will do everything you can to make them as happy as possible.

Your tenderness, compassion, sympathy, patience and understanding, combined with the fact that a happy home life is your greatest joy, will help to ensure that you aim for perfect rapport with your offspring. And the intuition bequeathed to you by the Moon will enable you to communicate on the deepest level.

By becoming more in tune with your inner being you will also appreciate that there is a time when you need to let go of your children, once they start to grow up and have lives of their own. Needless to say, this is sometimes a very hard thing for you to do! There is a side to your nature which enjoys having people lean on you, for you are such a protective soul – but that side can also be far too clinging!

In these times of escalating unemployment, homelessness, drug problems and HIV, think of the positive side of being able to communicate on that deepest level with your children. Try to ensure that there is always mutual trust between you for then you will know that you're being the best of all possible parents.

COPING WITH LIFE AFTER BREAK-UPS OR BEREAVEMENTS

It is never easy for anyone to cope with either of these issues. Since you are one of the most sentimental star signs, with that amazingly retentive memory which makes it hard for you to forget the past, it can be doubly difficult.

In addition, because you are such a hoarder of memorabilia you can sometimes land yourself with a real tear-jerking experience by reviewing the past. It can be all too easy for you to fall into a depression.

However, by communicating on a really deep level with your Inner Self – perhaps through the meditation technique which you will find on page 69 – you will gain an inner strength which helps you to remember those special, happy moments with affection. While your memories will naturally still be tinged with sadness, they will not deflate your spirits in a negative way.

LIFESTYLE, HEALTH AND DIET

The Cancer lifestyle will often revolve around your home life – not just because you are so domesticated, but simply because your greatest pleasures tend to involve being with the people closest to you in the cosy atmosphere where you live.

It's usually when you're not especially happy with your domestic life that you break out and indulge yourself in a variety of different interests. That is, of course, a generalisation and I can think of at least two domestically contented Cancerians who are active sports lovers, playing tennis early in the mornings before they go to their offices.

However, because you are so easily influenced by how you are feeling at any given moment, and since your moods fluctuate so much, you will benefit tremendously when you learn to balance your outer and your inner life. Yoga and meditation are perfect ways for you to do this, for the stillness you will achieve within will enable you to overcome any outward feelings of depression or insecurity or simply the feeling that you have got out of bed on the wrong side on a particular morning!

Sometimes, if you have read a lot about the influence of the Moon, you automatically assume that around Full Moon time you will sink into a horrendous depression. You then start to make not only your own life a drag but everyone else's as well – so that has to stop forthwith! Being at one with your Inner Self and appreciating the joy of feeling peaceful and calm inside will enable you to rise above such thoughts, so that you use the power of the Moon at all times to energise you and make you more creative, loving and intuitive.

It is wonderful for you to be near the water, whether it's walking along a seashore in the moonlight or simply sitting near a river or lake, and your favourite choice for a home could also reflect this. Sailing, fishing and swimming are all ideal Cancerian leisure activities, as are listening to romantic music and cooking wonderful meals for your family and friends. Among the alternative health therapies offered these days you may find yourself becoming increasingly interested in Spiritual Healing and Ayurvedic Medicine. The I Ching, Feng Shui and Dowsing may also be among your free-time interests. And you can certainly put your compassionate ways to very good use doing some kind of social work or hospital visiting, or perhaps even being a foster parent.

Your lifestyle, health and diet are all linked together and it's important that you recognise the benefits of a positive approach towards your mind, body and spirit. Since astrologically Cancer rules not only the breasts but also the stomach and digestive system, remember that what you eat will have a great bearing on how you feel. Sometimes you have a tendency to indulge yourself too much with foods which can have a disastrous effect on your stomach – especially as there is also a tendency for you to put on much too much weight around this area! Cancerians who over-indulge can also end up looking quite moon-faced as well as having too many bulges everywhere else!

Listen to your inner voice and you will definitely start to appreciate the benefits of a well-balanced diet and to feel greater peace and tranquillity within you.

GROWING OLD GRACEFULLY

Growing old gracefully for a typical Cancerian, whether male or female, will very much depend on how you feel about yourself and where you live. The older you get, the more important it is too for you to feel at home in the right sort of ambience.

You will still be very attached to family and possessions, but by understanding yourself more you will have developed the ability to let go of people and things when necessary without feeling sad or depressed.

Accept that there are bound to be times when your emotions fluctuate from highs to lows, and you won't get panicky about Full Moons or sulk if your favourite child or grandchild sometimes doesn't have the time to come and visit you. No longer will you fear your own inner world, or cling for far too long to old routines because you're frightened of what the future may hold, for you will have greater security within. And growing old gracefully can be a time when you're even more determined to offer your services to others less fortunate than yourself.

How To Get In Touch With The Inner You

At the beginning of this book I suggested that one way to understand your Inner Self more is to think of it as a Little Child, and as a Cancer you will enjoy nurturing this little child and shielding it from problems.

Your own particular form of meditation (see opposite) will be very helpful for you as it will help you to rise above any negative feelings or self-doubts.

Of course, you may already have your own meditation technique, and whatever is good for you is all right. It is the meditation itself which brings you the benefits.

Then each morning while you are washing or brushing your teeth, look at yourself in the mirror and affirm to yourself with feeling and conviction:

I will use my intuition to help others without being possessive or over-sentimental

The more you learn to understand your Inner Self, the easier it will be to understand that in some ways you can sometimes be

The Cancer Meditation

Choose a quiet place so that no one can disturb you. Sit comfortably on the floor in a cross legged position (or, if this is not comfortable, on a chair), close your eyes and visualise yourself sitting by a lake or the seashore. Concentrate on the point which lies between your eyebrows, and think of this point as your Divine centre as you sink into a meditative state. If you like you can imagine there is a New Moon (since the Moon does rule your sign) shining right there, and let its rays spread outward so that it fills your whole body with love and spreads out even further to fill the whole universe with that same love. Feel the love washing over you, like the waters of the lake or the soft waves of a gentle sea, and let your heart fill with the inner strength needed for your daily life, combined with the compassion and sensitivity which makes you who you are. If thoughts drift into your mind just let them float on by. Let the rays of the Moon waft over for you for approximately twenty minutes, at the end of which open your eyes gently.

Try to do this twice a day. You will soon start to find your intuition and perception are enhanced and that you feel an even stronger sense of purpose in life. You will soon know instinctively when your twenty minutes are up.

almost like a psychic sponge, taking in everything you feel, both negative and positive. And you will realise that by taking a more positive view of both yourself and the universe you will be even more special.

YOUR PERSONAL GUIDE TO THE FUTURE

By following the advice offered in this chapter you will understand and know yourself much better, which in turn means you will be able to enjoy even more fulfilling relationships in your emotional and your working life. It's not that you will suddenly become totally different, and be less home-loving and sentimental, but your attitude to your life and the way you live it *will* change. Your mood swings will be less intense, so you will be able to deal with the ups and downs of life in our times in an easier way.

You won't feel so much need to creep into that protective shell. And you won't allow yourself to sink in a sea of negative emotions, or to suffocate loved ones by possessively refusing to allow them to get on with their own lives. No more self-pity! No more hanging on to the past because you fear what is still to come! Your material security will still be an important factor in your life, but your inner security will be paramount.

You will have learnt that even in dark times there is always a light ahead, and that when you're truly in touch with your inner voice your life can be transformed in the most positive way for your mind, body and soul.

Positive Outlooks

★ Having the ability to see deep within
★ Giving unconditional love
★ Enjoying real domesticated bliss
★ Becoming more emotionally secure
★ Being resourceful and practical
★ Having powerful emotions
★ Being amazingly sensitive, kind and compassionate

Possible Pitfalls

★ Dwelling too much in the past
★ Still being possessive
★ Being ultra-sensitive to atmosphere
★ Being too self-protective or fearful
★ Being too concerned with material security
★ Remaining much too moody
★ Letting melancholia fly in the window
★ Being overly vulnerable

For the typical Cancer the idea of change in any form can be somewhat awe-inspiring and daunting. But by getting to know and understand the Inner You will gain so much peace of mind that you have no need to be worried. Your own special voyage of self-discovery will be one of the most wonderful experiences you have ever known.

Leo

☆

JULY 22 – AUGUST 21

Leo is the fifth sign of the Zodiac. You are a Masculine, Fixed, Positive sign, the second of the Fire signs. The Sun is your planetary ruler and your planetary symbol is the Lion.

With your sunny personality, charisma, personal magnetism, warmth, strong sense of self, generosity and creativity, you are one of the most dynamic, extrovert, romantic, lovable, larger than life and powerful personalities in the Zodiac – although perhaps at times you are also the most egotistical! Proud in the extreme, ambitious, bold and often aristocratic, you thrive on being praised not only for who you are but also for what you do. Yet, interestingly enough, for someone who on the surface appears to be amazingly strong you have a hidden vulnerability and child-like innocence which is very similar to that of Aries. Perhaps there is even more of the child within you – the child who smiles with joy when the sun is shining and weeps sad tears when the sky is grey and the rain pours down.

Leo rules the heart so it's not surprising that 'heart-warming' and 'heartfelt' are adjectives which can be applied so truthfully to you. With the typical Leo everything really does come from your heart. If you don't feel good about someone or something it is often quite hard for you to give of your best. You can also be quite bossy and domineering and as stubborn as any Taurus, with a know-it-all quality to match Sagittarius and the ability to roar as loudly as your symbol, the Lion.

But it is your Leo heart, that very essence of your being, which cries out to be loved and to give love and which is the dominating factor of your sign. A Leo without love of any kind in his or her life can be a sorry sight for everything you do is felt so deeply through your heart. If you're involved in any kind of creative work these heartfelt emotions invariably show in your achievements. This shows in the work of Debussy, Shelley and Tennyson, George Bernard Shaw and Alfred Hitchcock, as it also does in the brilliant character portrayals of Robert De Niro and Dustin Hoffman.

As a fiery Leo you need to feel inwardly that you are shining as brightly as the Sun, your ruling planet. It's not necessarily material success that you strive for (although with your inherent love of luxury and often extravagant and over-generous ways this cannot be ruled out) but you have to admit that you probably do want to be a star. It's not easy for a typical Leo to take anything less than first place in anything, for you thrive on being the leader – Leo the Lion, King of the Jungle and regal ruler of the Zodiac. But with so many job losses and increases in the cost of living in the 1990s you may sometimes have to forego that 'first place'.

Obviously, in any astrology book one can only generalise, and perhaps your own personal horoscope contains so many diverse planetary aspects that your Leo personality is overshadowed and nobody would suspect you were a Leo. But that is only speculation. Meanwhile, even if you don't have a mane-like head of Leonine hair to toss, you're probably one of the easiest signs to pick out in a crowd.

It is the sparkling and sunny side of your sign which so often makes it easier for you to adjust to changes which the outside world may foist upon you. You have an inborn ability to see the positive side of life, especially when you accept that sometimes it's only fair to let other people have a chance to shine as leaders in their own way too.

All of us have an outer personality and an inner one. In your case learning to understand the Inner You can have wonderfully beneficial results. Later in this chapter you will find your very own meditation technique and affirmation to help you do this. Meanwhile, it will help for you to think of your inner personality rather like a little child. That little child deep down is a warm and trusting little soul who longs to show the world how wonderful he or she is; although sometimes your outer personality finds it terribly difficult to cope with excessive Leo pride and a deep fear of failure.

One of the major advantages of communicating with your Inner Self is that you will learn to believe in yourself on a higher, more spiritual plane. It won't be so important for you to show your renowned Leo ego to the rest of us and to seek quite so relentlessly for approval and acclaim from others. You will know from within that you can be anything you want to be, including being a star on every level, but without having to prove it quite so obviously.

Meanwhile, the Outer You is sometimes so concerned with how you project yourself and how others see you that you forget to nurture your inner being. It can exhaust you at times; it's like continually being on a stage, giving so much of yourself. Unlike Cancer, the sign which precedes yours, the very thought of sinking into a sloth of depression is alien to the typical Leo – although if you're totally honest you will probably have to admit that you can at times become horribly lazy! And sometimes you set yourself almost impossibly high standards and then feel so dejected if you don't meet them.

Sometimes it is hard to convince you of the importance of learning about the Inner You. You're so often used to living life in the fast lane and projecting your sparkling personality that you don't even believe there could be a slightly different you hidden away inside. But the idea of a little personal self-analysis on the deepest possible level could also be exciting to you, and excitement and adventure are always appealing to the Lion of the Zodiac. Interestingly enough, Carl Jung and Aldous Huxley were both Leos; so too are Robert Redford, Sean Penn, Princess Anne, Danny La Rue and Jackie Onassis.

Creating the right balance between your outer and your inner personality isn't always the easiest thing in the world. As a Leo you are a fantastically loyal and devoted friend, a determined campaigner for everything in which you believe, a positive thinker, and someone who is possessed with infinite courage and strength – all qualities which are so important in these changing times. But one of the hardest things to deal with for so many people born under Leo is letting someone else take centre stage, so perhaps it will help you to understand the reason for this by realising that you truly are a child at heart, wanting to be reassured and cared for.

We all have something of our opposite sign in us, and while it's unlikely you could be as unconventional or unpredictable as Aquarius there are certainly times when you want to feel free and unfettered, just as Aquarians feel. No lion likes to feel imprisoned in a cage, and you hate to feel imprisoned in any way at all. When you do, the negative side of your personality creates someone who is more of a ruthless roaring dictator than a playful pussy cat or clown – Napoleon and Mussolini were both Leos.

Mind, body and soul – they all go together. And while you're a leader of leaders when you want to be, amazingly enough you're often innocently unaware of that great hidden potential which can make you even more lovable and able to combat even the most difficult challenges.

Positive and Negative, black and white, Yin and Yang, they all complement each other. Finding the right balance can bring you greater love and admiration from other people without your feeling you have to shout from the rooftops that Leo really *is* a star!

PATHWAYS TO SUCCESS IN THE 1990s

★ Be self-possessed and self-confident – but never too self-effacing.

★ Always combine your Leonine authority with sensitivity, and you will shine even more.

★ Resolve that exaggeration, extravagance and egotism will be things of the past.

★ Love and respect that little child within you, and you won't crave those words of praise from other people quite so much.

★ Listen to the words of Thomas Fuller who wrote: 'Let not thy will roar when thy power can but whisper'.

★ Do everything from the heart, but always remember not to be *too* trusting.

Your Ruling Planet . . . The Sun

One of the major influences on a male or female Leo is your planetary ruler. With the powerful Sun as the ruler of Leo it is no surprise that you are such a forceful and shining personality, for the Sun represents the cosmic masculine life force.

Sun worship has existed for centuries as a religious tradition. In mythology the Greek Apollo, Hermes and Dionysus were all said to be his descendants, as too was Osiris for the Egyptians and Abraham for the ancient Hebrews. They each represented the Heavenly Father on the earth, guarding the secret wisdoms. Apollo was the son of Zeus and in the fifth century BC he was linked with the strength, purity and light of the Sun; it is said that when he killed a snake that snake represented the dark, cold winter which ended because of the power of his blazing beauty. Apollo governed the seasons, watched over the herds and flocks, and was the god of agriculture. He was also said to be the first victor in the Olympic Games, and to symbolise the highest force of Man. No wonder so many of you are such born leaders!

In ancient Oriental traditions there was also a female Sun, and Japanese ruling clans said they were descended from a supreme Sun Goddess, Omikami Amaterasu. Among the ancient Arabs the Sun was also a Goddess; the Celts had a Sun Goddess whom they called Sulis, from the word 'suil' meaning both 'eye' and 'sun'; the Germans called her Sunna and the Norwegians Sol. In Britain, the Sun Goddess known as Sul, Sol or Sulis was worshipped at Silbury Hill, Avebury. So the Leo leadership is no less strong in the 'fairer sex'!

In the 1990s we have had more sun-spots, and more holes in the ozone layer which have increased the burning power of the Sun in often detrimental ways. The Sun is such a vital cosmic force, and with this powerful planet as your ruler it's also important for you to recognise and respect your own power.

In the body the Sun relates to the heart, spine, circulatory system, spleen and glands and the powerful life force which helps to make you such a strong and charismatic sign.

Every sign has its own particular colour or colours, and those particularly associated with you are orange, yellow and gold.

The symbol of the Sun is a circle with a dot in the middle, representing vitality and the ego. The symbol of Leo is the Lion, the king of beasts, which throughout history has been used as a mystical symbol. In ancient days the corona of the Sun was depicted as a lion's mane, and at one time the Summer Solstice occurred in the sign of Leo.

THE INNER CHALLENGE – THE OUTER CHANGE

There are sure to be some areas of your life which don't turn out exactly as you would like, always supposing that you are humble enough to admit such a thing!

If you're a typical Leo you are often so used to being the star turn that it becomes hard for you to step down from the limelight. But when you take the time and trouble to listen to your inner voice you will understand and accept that life can go on quite happily without your trying to control it, and that you will still enjoy it too.

The following areas will all be important to you in one way or another, and the great part of learning more about your Inner Self in relation to your sign is that you can achieve more contentment and fulfilment.

RELATIONSHIPS

When it comes to love your inner personality usually reflects your outer persona but in an even more romantic and idealistic way. The outer Leo thrives on love; a world without love would be a very sorry place for you. You want to give *and* receive it in a flamboyant, dramatic and extremely passionate way. You can also be amazingly conceited, determined to convince the object of your affections that you're the best lover they ever had.

However, underneath the surface of your often brash, extrovert and magnanimous personality beats a gentle heart of gold which is yearning for a special soulmate to transform your life into pure bliss of the most ethereal kind. Pure love really is what makes your own personal world go round, and you will do anything in the world to prove your deepest emotional feelings to the right partner. The little child within you is amazingly vulnerable when your deepest romantic feelings are stirred up, which is why it's also important to understand who you are and what you're really looking for.

The Outer Leo is so often tempted by what seems like love through someone who fits the physical requirements of your ideal lover – and who praises you to the hilt and is therefore the perfect

---

The Outer You   is fiercely attracted to passionate Aries; is aroused sensually by Taurus; enjoys flirting with Gemini; loves Cancer's home-cooked meals; sees Leo coming from a mile away; dislikes Virgo's need to analyse; enjoys the social life with Libra; finds sexy Scorpio almost *too* much; sees life as fun with Sagittarius; resents Capricorn's materialistic ways; is not usually ready for the cool and unemotional ways of Aquarius; enjoys showing romantic Pisces the high-life.

The Inner You   with Aries it's like two little children in love; finds security and stillness with an evolved Taurus; is able to *talk* about love in a surface way with Gemini; also loves those home-cooked meals, but is wary of Cancer's moods; recognises and is amused by Leo's mirror image; understands that Virgo too has insecurities; enjoys being partners with peaceful Libra; realises that Scorpio has deep emotions as well as passion; makes life a big adventure with Sagittarius; appreciates that security with Capricorn doesn't have to be boring; tries to understand that Aquarius needs to feel free; thinks that romance could last for ever with Pisces.

audience! But the Inner Leo knows deep down that fiery passion can also burn away too fast, and that beauty really is only skin deep. You know that you're as romantic as any Pisces, as innocently idealistic as Aries, and as needy for the perfect partner as Libra.

By delving deeper into your inner being you will find greater self-confidence, and there will be far less conflict between the more obvious needs of your Outer You and the romantic yearnings of the Inner You. You will also be inspired to learn more about the inner feelings of all the people who figure in your life so that *all* your relationships become more rewarding.

CAREERS AND BUSINESS

Both male and female Leos want to be the stars of the show, no matter where your talents lie, and that is your goal whether you care to admit it or not! Whether you're a boss (and needless to say not *every* Leo can be at the top) or an employee, respect and praise for your efforts are major Leo requirements. You also consider it imperative to respect and admire the people you work for and with.

It's also true that when you are involved in a career or business situation which fulfils your creative needs (and which even makes getting up in the morning a thing of pleasure and not a bore) your material expectations and desires become less important. But combined with your spurts of energy there is often the lazy side of your nature which means you hate to go without your moments of rest.

Of course, it can also become a problem if your goal is purely creative satisfaction and you're not too concerned about your pay cheque. If you are one of those typically over-generous and extravagant Leos who finds it extraordinarily hard to balance your books you could easily be out of pocket rather too often.

You will work long and hard when you are doing something you enjoy, sometimes so hard that you don't even give yourself enough time to rest and relax. While it's true that there is a lazy streak attached to Leos, it certainly won't show when you're serious about your work.

Your flamboyant personality invariably does express itself in your work, and Andy Warhol, Arnold Schwarzenegger and Mick Jagger are all born under your sign, with Madonna surely the most flamboyant of all!

When you learn to communicate more with the Inner You, you will also realise that as long as you totally believe in yourself and your endeavours (without becoming horribly conceited, of course) it really isn't so important to have people fawning over you and telling you how wonderful you are. It's always pleasing to receive compliments, and I'm certainly not suggesting that you should go out of your way to avoid them. But when you have complete faith in your talents and abilities you won't *need* anyone else to confirm it to you, and you can concentrate on other issues.

In many ways you're as much of a perfectionist as any Virgo, but in your case it's not necessarily that you worry you're not good enough. If you're a typical Leo your outward projection that you know you're good seems to conflict with an inner vulnerability that needs constant reassurance, which is all the more reason to achieve the right balance between your inner and outer personality.

Leo careers include acting, fashion, film directing, public relations, theatre management, art, teaching, and being the head of a company. But the main criterion is that you have the opportunity to project your sparkling personality to best advantage in the careers which fulfil you the most.

How Do You Handle Decisions?

There will always be decisions to be made in life, and as a Fixed Fire sign you often make them fairly quickly. But since you consider yourself the true leader of the Zodiac you also expect everyone else to fall in with your decisions whether or not they are in agreement. Bossy, domineering – who, you?!

By communicating more with your inner being you will start to realise and accept that you can't have everything you want, even if you do feel you should. And once you accept that you don't always have to be the King or Queen ruling over your subjects you might find that it can be very pleasant to let someone else make some decisions for a change – as long as you're not totally opposed to them of course!

The meditation technique and affirmation which you will find later in this chapter will enable you to understand and deal with the deep emotions and insecurities which help to make you the way you are. Once you've appreciated their benefit you will also learn to let go of your ego sufficiently to ensure that your decision making is no longer simply linked to what *you* want, but also to what can be good for everyone else who is involved with each particular issue.

How Do You Handle Conflicts?

Once you start to change your attitude over decision making by listening to your inner voice it will also be easier for you to handle conflicts because you won't have to have the major conflict of all – you versus your ego!

Meanwhile, you can so often behave like a lion roaring in the jungle preparing to launch his attack on his prey. It is invariably in conflicts that the dictatorial side of your personality comes to the fore (Mussolini and Napoleon ride again), and your ego is positively overpowering as you throw off negative vibes like a volcano ready to erupt! Being criticised in any way at all invariably either throws you into deep dejection or starts a full-scale war attacking your opponent's intelligence!

But that sweet, lovable, sparkling Leo is never too far below the surface, so listen to the little child within you. And always remember that the power of your planetary ruler, the Sun, is such a vital life force and fills you with so much positive energy, strength and belief in yourself as a positive human being that you simply don't need to waste your time on unnecessary conflicts.

When you allow your enthusiasm and joie de vivre to prevail over other problems, and you utilise your power to overcome conflicts rather than create them or make them worse, you will find much more of that inner peace which is so important in these turbulent times.

Your opposite sign of Aquarius tends to avoid conflicts by being totally cool and detached, and there is no way a typical Leo could ever do that! You feel things far too passionately both outwardly and inwardly. But the beautiful part of being more in touch with your innermost feelings is that you will start to achieve a state of calmness and relaxation which will make it impossible for anyone to really hurt you.

You As A Parent

Because you are so much of a child at heart yourself – almost like a playful clown with a heart of gold – you can be the most wonderful parent in the world. You genuinely love children and relate to them especially well.

However, your Leonian love of the limelight sometimes means that you have a hard job allowing your children their chance to shine as they grow up and develop their own unique personalities and talents. It's not that you're not proud of them – far from it, you revel in their creative attributes even if you *are* convinced they've inherited them all from you! It's simply that you really do find it hard to take that second place.

By becoming more in tune with your inner voice you will find it much easier to relinquish your own desire for stardom. You will enjoy watching your children grow from infancy to adulthood, making your Leo kingdom complete and your home your palace. Of course there will always be times when you do need to lay down the law and be the dominant father or mother figure. But your offspring will know that you are a parent they can both love and respect, which is more important than ever in these times when unrest seems to prevail in the world.

Coping With Life After
Break-Ups Or Bereavements

The more you are at one with your Inner Self, the easier it will be for you to cope with life after break-ups and bereavements.

However, where emotional break-ups are concerned a great deal always seems to depend on whether you initiated the split or whether it was forced upon you. It's so hard for your Leo pride to accept that you could be at fault or found lacking in any way. That's why believing in yourself wholeheartedly deep inside, without any airs and graces, will enable you to rise above even the most difficult of break-ups by believing and accepting that perhaps they were meant to be – unless of course they were as a result of your being the villain!

You give your love so wholeheartedly to the people closest to you that when you have to cope with bereavement it is really hard. But that same inner voice and that strong revitalising force of the Sun will work together to give you the strength to move forward and not dwell for too long in the past.

LIFESTYLE, HEALTH AND DIET

The Leo lifestyle is often flamboyant, invariably extremely social, and almost never dull. You love entertaining and make a brilliant host or hostess. Since your home is definitely your castle you love showing it off, for you are as proud of your possessions as you are of yourself and the people who are closest to you.

Entertainment in all its forms is a vital part of your lifestyle, and the creative side of your nature wants to be fulfilled by seeing all the latest plays and films. But Leo the lion can be very lazy when it comes to any form of more active exercise, and you can also sometimes be too keen on the good life without giving yourself enough time to relax. Aromatherapy can make you feel wonderful and you're probably always in the mood for a really good massage. Those of you who yearn to express some unfulfilled creative talents might like to join an Art Workshop, or a Drama Therapy course or amateur dramatics group – Leo is often a 'natural' actor or actress.

One of the benefits of getting more in touch with your Inner Self is that you will start to find that rest and relaxation are not always simply an excuse for you to be lazy. Rather, they are a chance for your mind to unwind and your whole being to re-energise itself in a powerful and positive way. You will find your own special meditation techniques and affirmations at the end of this chapter, and they will help you to find the inner peace which is becoming more and more important in the often turbulent 1990s.

To have the Sun as your planetary ruler is a wonderful asset, for by simply being in the sunshine and lapping up its beneficial rays you can gain so much. However, that doesn't mean lying in the sun for hours to get a wonderful tan when it is very hot, especially now that the ozone layer is becoming thinner all the time. Even if it's dull outside or the rain is pouring down you can always simply visualise the sun's rays pouring over and into you, filling you with positive energy.

Your lifestyle, health and diet are all linked together, and it's important to remember this so that you lead a balanced life in every way. It's all very well being a brilliant host or hostess and entertaining your guests with sumptuous food. But don't forget to eat properly when there is just you to cook for and it becomes easier to reach for the nearest can. And sometimes you enjoy too much rich food, so do watch your cholesterol level.

Astrologically Leo rules the heart, the spine and back, and the circulatory system. And because you invariably tend to live your life in the fast lane, enjoying every day to the full, there is a tendency that you can overdo things. By listening more to your inner voice and consequently allowing your intuition to tell you when it is time to slow down (as against slacking when you feel lazy!) you will help to avoid the risk of heart attacks and other heart diseases which can be a Leo problem as you start to grow older.

If you're a typical Leo you really *are* ruled by your heart and emotions. The lesson to learn is to balance those powerful heartfelt emotions with your mind so that your inner energy flow is positive. It's when this energy flow is out of balance that you become more egotistic, even more concerned with your outward life and out of sync with the real you. By nature you are certainly one of the most loving and generous signs but it has also been said that if you negate these emotions this can lead to the development of heart and circulatory problems – even more reason to go within and start to know yourself better. When your inner being is calm your outer personality will shine even more brightly and you will become increasingly popular with everyone else in your life without having to consciously project yourself as being a star.

GROWING OLD GRACEFULLY

Growing old gracefully for a typical Leo, whether male or female, will be interesting to see for it will be a time for you to slow down at least a little to avoid the risk of overstraining your Leo heart. It's also a time when, hopefully, you will know that taking second place once in a while doesn't signify the end of the world. Even if someone else's star is in the ascendant, it doesn't mean that you're any less of a star yourself.

But since you will always remain a child at heart, with a bountiful supply of mental and physical energy at your disposal, growing old with more understanding of your inner being can bring you infinite pleasures. You will never tire of being sociable, never lose that sunny, sparkling personality which is your trademark. And with a calmer, more tranquil approach to life you won't be quite so domineering any more! There will always be plenty you can do for others less fortunate than you. Simply by projecting positive thoughts and actions, with a smile on your Leo face, you can achieve so much – you'd be wonderful at helping to organise charity functions or collections.

Growing old gracefully for a Leo who has truly recognised how wonderful it is to give love to others, and has appreciated the blessing of the Sun's vital force within you, is something to look forward to and enjoy.

HOW TO GET IN TOUCH WITH THE INNER YOU

At the beginning of this book I suggested that one way to learn more about your Inner Self is to think of it as a little child. As a Leo this will not be difficult for you since you have such a fantastic ability to communicate well with children on every level in the outer world, and truly *are* such a child at heart.

Your own particular meditation and affirmation will make this inner communication even easier.

The Leo Meditation

Choose a quiet place so that no one can disturb you. Sit comfortably on the floor, in a cross-legged position (or, if this is not comfortable, on a chair), close your eyes and visualise the Sun, your ruler, as a wonderful golden light flowing upwards and outwards and all around you, engulfing you in a warm glow which spreads love and happiness in every part of your being. Feel this love growing and growing until it seems as though it is reaching out to all the corners of the world, bringing sunshine and happiness to all who need it. Let yourself sink slowly into a meditative state, basking in your feelings. If thoughts come into your mind, let them float gently by. At the end of approximately twenty minutes, start to visualise the sun beginning to sink low in the sky, bringing with it a wonderful sunset which fills you with immense peace.

Try to do this twice a day. You will soon start to find that your joie de vivre will become even stronger, and your feelings of love and generosity to others will also grow.

You may already have your own way of meditating, and that's fine. The important thing is that you recognise the benefits which meditation can bring you.

Then when you're washing or brushing your teeth each morning, look at yourself in the mirror and affirm to yourself with feeling and conviction:

I will unselfishly try to bring love and light to others in everything I do today

The more you understand your Inner Self, the easier it will be

for you to realise that your need for adulation from others has diminished because you have sufficient self-confidence deep within to know and appreciate your true worth. Because of this you will become an even more lovable personality.

YOUR PERSONAL GUIDE TO THE FUTURE

By following the advice offered in this chapter you will understand and know yourself much better, and will be able to have even more fulfilling relationships in your emotional and working life.

You won't suddenly change overnight – become introvert instead of extrovert, or lose your Leo sparkle – but your ego will be less demanding and you will have developed a new kind of strength: the strength to recognise your weaknesses. And you will appreciate each day more, for you will have an even greater understanding of how beautiful life can be with your own personal rays of sunshine to enhance the innermost part of your being. You will want to give more of yourself to help other people who can benefit from your positive input, perhaps talking to teenagers about the problems of growing up in today's world and inspiring them to develop their own creative talents as you have done.

The playful Leo clown will still at times need to be admired by other people but deep down you will have much greater belief in the magic of your dreams and in the longevity of your relationships with the people you care for most. And if you can inspire others to believe in their dreams too and do something positive about them – then you really can feel proud of your achievements!

Positive Outlooks

★ Enjoying a calmer way of life
★ Harnessing your emotions better

Possible Pitfalls

★ Still trying to dominate. . .
★ . . .and still roaring like a lion!

★ Balancing mind, body
  and soul as one
★ Feeling sunshine
  radiating through you
★ Letting your energy
  flow in harmony
★ Enjoying giving and
  receiving love
★ Accepting your
  limitations
★ Trusting life to the
  full

★ Remaining too
  obsessed with ego
★ Being too flamboyant
★ Being too lazy to look
  within
★ Selfishly wanting
  more
★ Being an *over-*
  achiever
★ Fearing failure

For the typical Leo, so often fixed in ideas and opinions, looking deep within may seem daunting if you like yourself the way you are and feel that's good enough. But the challenge of getting to know and understand the Inner You so that you can really be a star on mind, body *and* soul level is something you will always cherish once you've taken those first steps on your own special journey.

Virgo

— ☆ —

AUGUST 22 – SEPTEMBER 21

Virgo is the sixth sign of the Zodiac, often referred to as 'the sign of service'. You are a Feminine, Mutable, Negative sign, the second of the Earth signs. Mercury, planet of communication, is your planetary ruler, and your planetary symbol is the Virgin.

An analytical, discriminating, alert, bright, versatile, logical, meticulous, neat, tidy, dedicated and determined human being, that's you – one of the most dependable people one could ever wish to know, for you are amazingly conscientious and responsible and usually far too modest! You have a wonderfully witty sense of humour, which sparkles brilliantly when you allow it to shine forth. And shine forth it must if you are going to find content and fulfilment in the changing times of the 1990s, with their ever increasing reports of wars, famines, drug abuse and other tragedies.

Oscar Wilde wrote, 'Better to take pleasure in a rose than to put its root under a microscope', and I've often felt that was a perfect maxim for you. The world is changing all around us very fast, and it's so important for you to appreciate who you are and what you can do to make it a better place. Some of you have taken that description of 'the sign of service' too literally and tend to forget that you *are* allowed to enjoy your life to the full. Being needed is all very well, but you need to look after *you* as well.

Obviously, in any astrology book one can only generalise, and perhaps your own personal horoscope contains so many diverse planetary aspects that your Virgo personality is overshadowed and nobody would even guess you were a Virgo. But that is pure speculation, and meanwhile it's all too easy for you to take upon your shoulders all the worries of the world.

Once you start to think about yourself in a more positive way you will realise that all your marvellous assets can help you to adapt brilliantly to the fast changes going on around you. It should actually be easier for you than for many of the rest of us to know what is best for you and everyone else in your life, for by using your powers of discrimination you will be able to visualise how things are going to turn out, rather than worry that you could feel let down.

However, sometimes it's not easy for you to project the most positive of images as you can be as shy and timid as your opposite sign of Pisces. Greta Garbo was Virgo! Since you share the same planetary ruler as Gemini – Mercury, planet of communication – it's about time you woke up to the fact that you're invariably highly intelligent, articulate, intellectually extremely alert *and* fun to be with. Mercury does not encourage dullness!

All of us have an outer personality and an inner one. And in your case, learning to understand the Inner You can be one of the most valuable lessons you could possibly have. Later in this chapter you will find your very own meditation technique and affirmation to help you to do this. Meanwhile, it will help for you to think of your inner personality rather like a little child. That little Virgo child deep down really *does* want to have a good time, but sometimes your outer personality is stuck so much on a material level that a great deal of what you feel and say is based on that.

I'm not asking you to suddenly change your personality overnight, but I think it's about time you recognised that appreciating yourself isn't a sin, unless you start to overdo it to the point of excessive vanity – and I don't think you're likely to do that.

Virgo is the sign of the critic – and yes, you're utterly brilliant at criticising yourself and everyone else. However, sometimes you lack sufficient breadth of vision, and interestingly enough you are never able to deal with things too well if someone decides to criticise *you* for a change. At this point you will vehemently deny that you have any faults worth mentioning, and maybe you truly believe that you *are* a paragon of virtue.

Meanwhile, if you will only take the time and trouble to learn more about your innermost needs and feelings you will save yourself a whole lot of worrying, for if you're a typical Virgo you will probably find it hard to deny that you *do* worry too much. This is also not good for your health, as you will read later in this chapter.

What you generally need more than anything else is to believe wholeheartedly in yourself as a unique individual who is capable of fulfilling your innermost dreams. I have a bookmark I bought in New York which says 'Believe in the Magic of Your Dreams'. Take it as your motto, Virgo, and make those words happen for you. By going deep within so that you begin to see the inter-relatedness of everything you really will find your life becoming more rewarding. Think of Sophia Loren, a Virgo who rose from the back streets of Naples to become an international movie star and obviously did believe in the magic of her dreams.

Naturally, creating the perfect balance between your outer and your inner personality isn't always the easiest thing in the world. As a Virgo, you've inevitably trained yourself extremely well as far as routines, schedules and disciplines are concerned. And per-haps the idea of taking time off to expand your vision through somehow learning more about the Inner You and restructuring your existing lifestyle doesn't seem quite on. But come on, Virgo, the world isn't going to end simply because you're not around to hold the fort if someone needs you. Besides, the world of the 1990s is different from that of the 1960s, 1970s and 1980s. We're not just reaching the end of a century, but the end of a millennium!

Every time you feel you're becoming too much of a worry-wart, think about your opposite sign in the Zodiac – romantic, dreamy Pisces, who really does believe in magic. We all have something of our opposite signs within us, and we have something to learn from them too. Start to love yourself unconditionally, for feeling good about oneself is a wonderful way to feel.

Positive and Negative, Yin and Yang, we need to have both, and once you start to feel the balance between the Outer and the

Inner You, life in the 1990s will take on a whole new perspective. You will begin to revel in your strengths and learn to overcome any weaknesses that might have sent you scuttling for cover in the past.

PATHWAYS TO SUCCESS IN THE 1990s

★ Stop analysing why you can't do something, and analyse not only why you *can* . . . but why it's going to work!
★ Remember that fear usually goes to the stomach, and ask yourself why you should want to give your stomach problems.
★ Believe in yourself – it's the best way to make everyone else believe in you too.
★ And stop being so concerned about what other people might say from now on.
★ Since you have such a great sense of humour, resolve to use it even more.
★ See things through your heart . . . not simply with your mind.

YOUR RULING PLANET . . . Mercury, Winged Messenger of the Gods

One of the major influences on a male or female Virgo is your planetary ruler. Mercury, which rules your sign in addition to that of Gemini, represents your rational mind and demonstrates the strength of your mental qualities, and it has always been known as that Winged Messenger of the Gods. Its ability to enhance your quick comprehension and your intellectual and analytical prowess is undisputed by anyone who has spent very much time with you. But since you are an Earth sign, whereas Gemini is Air, its mercurial influence on you tends to be towards a very pragmatic and realistic approach to life. You have the ability to arrange just about anything extremely well and, unlike Gemini, your Virgoan feet remain very much on the ground. While Gemini analyses, you prefer to organise.

Mercury was called Mercury by the Romans, but the Greeks called him Hermes, and the Egyptian name for him was Thoth.

The Greeks said he was older than their land, and he was often described as the first hermaphrodite, whose body was united with Aphrodite. The sign of Mercury is taken from the cross of Hermes, who was the god of the four elements, the four quarters of the earth, the four winds, and the equinoxes and solstices represented by Taurus, Leo, Scorpio and Aquarius. The cross of Hermes was sometimes shown as an Ankh (an Ancient Egyptian life charm) standing on a crescent symbolising the Moon who represented his mother. From this original symbol we get the more conventional sign of Mercury which is a circle with a cross below it and a crescent above.

In the body Mercury relates to the brain and to the respiratory and nervous systems. Because of this link with the nervous system it has been said that the B complex vitamins relate to Mercury.

There are some astrologers who feel that Vulcan (planet of thunder, and yet to be visible through a telescope) is the rightful ruler of Virgo. In Greek mythology, Vulcan was a lame God who possessed a brilliant mind, and it is definitely true that most people born under the sign of Virgo have incredibly good minds.

Every sign has its own particular colour or colours and the colours especially associated with you are navy, brown and dark grey, and sometimes yellow too. I've often noticed that people born under your sign tend to like dressing in these colours, using stripes and checks in the material. Blue is also associated with your planet, Mercury, and the soothing vibration of this colour helps to relax and heal the nervous system.

Your planetary symbol is the Virgin, and she is the only feminine figure in the Zodiac. In ancient times Virgo was worshipped as the Earth Goddess and was shown holding an ear of wheat, the symbol of fertility. Renaissance poets called her Astraea – 'Starry One' – and she was supposed to be the Goddess of Justice, and daughter of Jupiter and Themsis. Mythology has it that after the Golden Age she returned to the heavens because she was angry not to have her rules obeyed on Earth.

As a Virgo, with Mercury as your ruler and the Virgin as your symbol, you have an interesting challenge ahead of you. It is up to you to broaden your vision without losing either the purity of your beliefs or the brilliantly discriminating power of your intellect; and to learn to analyse in perhaps a more positive way.

Then you will be able to look at the times in which we live as a period to grow inwardly as well as outwardly, and to enjoy greater communication with your higher mind as well as to achieve your goals in the real world.

THE INNER CHALLENGE –
THE OUTER CHANGE

There are bound to be certain areas of your life which don't always work out exactly as you would like – Michael Jackson is a Virgo who has often appeared to worry too much about himself – but it's best not to be *too* self-critical. Of course, if you are a typical Virgo you probably have a list as long as your arm of the things you don't like about yourself. If you start by crossing off 'being overly self-critical' you can probably wipe off half the rest as well!

The following areas will all be important to you in one way or another, and if you're prepared to stop analysing and dissecting yourself for just a while and resolve to listen to what your inner voice might have to tell you, the rewards could be greater than you think.

RELATIONSHIPS

You can be an interesting blend of cynicism and naivety when it comes to relationships. Because you are so analytical you tend to dissect emotional issues far too much, yet just like your opposite sign of Pisces you will do everything in the world for the people you care for most. And your quiet, subdued outer image can suddenly project itself more like a volcano, which perhaps lends greater truth to the idea of Vulcan being one of your planetary rulers. You take relationships extremely seriously, and are usually very faithful. But you also have to be careful that your 'sign of service' tag doesn't mean you land yourself with lame dogs and end up being a martyr – with even more reasons to criticise yourself.

Deep down you often yearn to lose your cool and controlled image and become as fiery and passionate as Aries or Scorpio, but you worry and doubt yourself too much. However, if you are truly prepared to broaden your vision and visualise yourself with the perfect partner who will fulfil your deepest needs, and at the same time open up your heart and soul and let your inner voice have it's say, you really will be able to see the 'magic of your dreams'.

The following guide will help you to see the benefits of getting to know the Inner You when romance is involved!

The Outer You sees Aries as overpoweringly aggressive; criticises the stubborn ways of Taurus; finds Gemini much too flirtatious; thinks Cancer could worry almost more than you; finds Leo's vanity just too much to take; hates to admit that you have any Virgoan faults; isn't too sure about Libra's lazy, indecisive ways; tends to think the worst of Scorpio's sexy magnetism; feels that too much optimism is unwise for Sagittarius; relates well to Capricorn's pragmatic realism; tries too hard to analyse that one-off style of Aquarius; concentrates too much on that Piscean impracticality.

The Inner You feels life can be great fun with Aries; enjoys the sybaritic side of life with Taurus; appreciates long, interesting conversations with Gemini; remembers never to be too picky when Cancer sulks; learns to be less critical of Leo's flamboyant style; yearns to help Virgo unwind . . . together with you; appreciates Libra's quiet, unassuming charm; refuses to be intimidated by Scorpio's sexual techniques; discovers optimism with Sagittarius is far better than pessimism alone; relaxes in total security with Capricorn; realises that understanding Aquarius can be a unique experience; loves to be romantic with your opposite sign of Pisces.

By delving deeper into your inner being you will stop analysing and criticising so much, and find it easier to recognise and respect what you need from a romantic relationship in order for it to be successful. You need to feel you're giving something, but you also know that you need to be loved for yourself. So stop living quite so much on the material plane and get to know yourself better so that you will appreciate life more.

Learning more about the Inner You will inspire you to learn more about the inner feelings of everyone who is important in your life, so that all your relationships become even more rewarding.

CAREERS AND BUSINESS

Both male and female Virgoans are without doubt among the most hardworking signs of the Zodiac, yet again living up to your description as 'the sign of service'. You are invariably highly competent and capable at just about anything you are asked to undertake. If you're a typical Virgo you are probably thought of as totally indispensable by employers and colleagues alike, although no doubt you are far too modest to dare admit this possibility!

Being indispensable is certainly something to give you confidence in the 1990s, for with the economic state of the world – along with everything else – in continual fluctuation, so many people from the top down are losing their jobs every day. But you can achieve even more if you don't concentrate entirely on being the only perfectionist still to be found on Earth. Needless to say, you will probably always end up being the last one to leave your place of work most days, and that's fine as long as you truly enjoy what you're doing.

If you're not careful you tend to go about your chosen career a bit like a drudge, ploughing yourself wholeheartedly into your set routine and discipline, and almost refusing to allow too many sparks of creativity to burst to the surface for fear they might be leading you up the wrong path. You can be amazingly creative, Virgo, so listen to your Inner Self a little more and start to let your imagination flow freely. Don't hold it back in chains, even if you're not aiming for stardom.

A perfect eye for detail is a marvellous advantage, for it surely won't take you long to see when something is not working out well and for you to find a better way to deal with it. And think how much more successful you can be when you combine your positive characteristics and negate any negative ones!

It's often been said that people born under Virgo tend to hide their lights under bushels, working in the background and letting everyone else take the limelight. But the more you listen and take note of your needs, the more you will know that isn't always true. Leonard Bernstein, Henry Ford, Peter Sellers and Elia Kazan certainly didn't fall into that category, and neither do Jacqueline Bisset, Harrison Ford, Jeremy Irons or Raquel Welch. If Twiggy had simply thought of herself as a skinny working-class girl with no prospects, where would she be now? And if Sean Connery had focused solely on his Scots accent and was terrified at the very idea of Hollywood, we'd have missed some fantastic performances.

Don't let the feeling that you were born to serve prevent you from receiving your fair due. Fear of failure and insecurity about the future often make you worry too much about what you should be paid. You know you're worth what you put into your work, so just project that image on the people who are going to pay you. In the 1990s you can't just sit back and wait: People are far more inclined to trample all over each other to get a job, and a self-effacing Virgo would end up at the bottom of the pile.

Any kind of public service is ideally suited to you. And your eye for detail makes you an ideal accountant, book keeper, pharmacist, scientist, craftsman, draughtsman, statistician, teacher, doctor, nurse or psychologist, good at anything which involves health and hygiene, a top-class secretary, and a brilliant proof reader or anything else in the publishing field.

How Do You Handle Decisions?

There will always be decisions to be made in life, but the trouble with being a typical Virgo is that you are likely to worry so much and so long about what needs to be done that you end up as a bundle of nerves after a sleepless night.

It's all down to analysing everything in the finest detail yet
again, and because you can get in such a state about that you really
don't see the wood for the trees. Stop taking everything quite so
seriously when it doesn't warrant it. Take a deep breath, relax and
look at the overall picture of whatever it is that needs a decision.
Try to clear your mind of all the 'what ifs' that are sure to come
crowding in, and simply think about what is best for you or
whoever you're making the decision for at this particular
moment.

At this stage it would be wonderful if you could wander off to a
river, sit yourself down and simply watch the water flowing;
imagine it flowing through your mind, taking away all your
worries with it, leaving you with the clearness and clarity you
possess in abundance but which you tend to lose when you're
forced into a corner and panic! But you don't *need* to be by that
river: try visualising it instead.

How Do You Handle Conflicts?

When your attitude towards decision making starts to change you
will find conflicts easier to handle too, for so often the biggest
conflict is with yourself! If from an early age you have had a
magnified perception of yourself as being far less than perfect,
you're often going to play the martyr, with it's never ending sense
of duty. When you have to cope with conflicts you will so often
doubt that you're in the right.

It's not that by learning to go within and understand yourself
more that you suddenly will *always* be right! But loving yourself
more is certainly going to make it a whole lot easier to love
everyone else too, and perhaps lessen the need for certain
conflicts in the future.

If you're totally honest with yourself you must admit that you
often create unnecessary conflicts by being so picky, fussy – call it
what you will – and that your exacting ways can be quite a strain
on the more disorganised among us! Untidiness might drive you
crazy. You may look askance at someone eating the sort of food it
almost sends your stomach into spasm to think of. The extravagance of Leo is something you hate to contemplate. And the way

so many Scorpios flaunt their sexuality could turn you into even more of a prude. You don't really like your life to be disorganised in any way at all, or to be woken up by loud traffic outside your home, or anyone arriving late for an appointment. The list of your dislikes could be almost endless! But once you overcome some of your uncertainty about yourself you'll find most of these things are only annoyances which aren't worth creating conflicts about – even with yourself!

You As a Parent

Because you are such a caring person you will invariably do everything possible for your offspring, and will give them the best education you can afford. But don't make yourself into a long-suffering martyr who is determined to sacrifice everything for the sake of your children and then criticise every single thing they do. Always remember that, with times changing so fast, youngsters today really do have a different view of life.

Because of your fastidious views on health and diet, and your natural abhorrence of anything which could lead to sickness or any health-related problems, it will sometimes be hard for you not to worry about drug abuse, Aids, and all the other hazards of the current times. Try to be there to advise your children when they need you, but try also not to be the kind of parent who fusses over them so much that in the end they hide things from you – for then you're only going to worry more.

Conscientious and responsible, you can be a perfect parent; able to have an excellent rapport with your offspring, especially on an intellectual level. The influence of your ruler, Mercury, will ensure that communication need be no problem.

Coping With Life After
Break-ups or Bereavements

Once you've learnt to stop your mind creating worry after worry in your life through being more at one with your Inner You, you will also have learnt how to cope more easily with the really rough passages we all have to go through.

Coping with break-ups or bereavements isn't easy for anyone. But don't start finding reasons to blame yourself and fall into one of your horribly self-critical moods because things have gone wrong between you and the love of your life. And don't block yourself off from the thought of enjoying life again for fear of similar situations in the future – something which it is all too easy for you to do.

Somehow you often seem to find it hard to show your grief, hiding behind a placid exterior when deep down you want to cry your eyes out. But it really is all right to cry. In fact often it's the best release you could have, so don't hold back your emotions when inwardly you feel the time and place is right to let them go. You only risk increasing the chances of landing yourself in a stress situation.

The more positive you start to feel mentally, the more balanced you will feel emotionally. So while there can be times when you feel sadness and grief, you will still be able to see and feel some beauty around you too. The meditation and affirmation given later in this chapter will also help you to find that mind, body and soul balance.

LIFESTYLE, HEALTH AND DIET

The Virgo lifestyle is unlikely to contain too many excesses of any kind. The odd occasion when you might suddenly let your hair down and run wild is unlikely to do you very much harm, though, and could be lots of fun – within reason, of course!

Invariably you are dedicated to the well-being of your body. But that doesn't necessarily mean you are the most exercise-conscious of folk, unless it's going to be something which you feel fits into your schedule and can be rigorously carried out regularly. You're unlikely to be sitting at your desk and suddenly decide you could do with a good long walk or a game of tennis, for your devotion to duty tends to inhibit you from such thoughts.

Some of you are far more inclined to consider tackling a pile of ironing, patching up the tiles on the roof or doing some heavy-duty gardening as necessary features of your lifestyle. That's fine as long as you enjoy doing them, but it's not likely to soothe your perhaps already frazzled nerves if you don't! And it is so often those frazzled nerves which need more care and attention. The more you get to know the inner part of you, the more this will become apparent.

Of course, when duty calls there is no way a Virgo is not going to respond; but time off for leisure will actually enable you to deal with your duties, even those self-imposed ones, in a much more relaxed and pleasurable way. Since health is always one of your major interests, you might decide to involve yourself in learning about aromatherapy, herbal treatments or perhaps the Bach Flower Remedies. This would be a very positive move on two counts, for you might find it helps you not only to be of service in some way to other people but also to give yourself a treat at the same time.

Don't always be the last one to leave your place of work. Go out to movies, plays and concerts, have social evenings with friends, and think about *you*. You can still do your charity work, hospital visits, listening to the problems of your friends – but you can't afford to neglect yourself.

Your eating habits tend to be very healthy and diet-conscious for the most part, and I can't recall seeing many overweight Virgoans. However, your preoccupation with cleanliness can sometimes mean you're almost paranoid about seeing a caterpillar on a lettuce leaf, or you insist on going on holiday with far too large a medicine box because you fear that all those foreign foods are going to upset your tummy. Hypochondria is all too common among people born under your sign, and sometimes you almost create your own self-fulfilling prophecies. You worry so much about the contents of the food you're really enjoying that the poor old Virgo nervous system gets itself totally knotted up, and sure enough your stomach starts to rebel. All the more reason to calm yourself inwardly and know that you're going to be all right.

Virgo rules the nervous system and intestines, especially the small intestine, and also the digestive tract. So it's not surprising that those of you who tend to worry about things even more than the average Virgoan can often suffer from bowel and stomach problems, often related to your nervous system. It's therefore extremely important for you to keep a positive slant on life, and not give way to negatives and self-doubts.

Your mind, body and spirit are inexorably entwined, and there really is no need for you to upset the delicate workings of your nervous system when you see how to appreciate the qualities of your life. Resolve that from now on you will no longer become irritable at the slightest little mistake, fuss irrationally over someone being five minutes late, or give yourself a headache going over and over the same self-doubts which rise up inside.

GROWING OLD GRACEFULLY

Growing old gracefully for you will hopefully mean just that – a time when you can stop trying to carry the worries of the world upon your shoulders, and live neither in the past nor the future but in the now.

It's not that you are suddenly going to eliminate the possibility of worrying about anything ever again, but you may be able to look upon little worries rather like naughty little children, just there to test your patience and see if you are going to react. And since you will be wiser as well as older, you will know that, just like the river flowing by, those worries will flow by in the same way and cease to create dramas in your life.

The critical side of your nature can be brilliantly adapted to writing your own reviews on the programmes you see on TV, or sending letters to your favourite newspaper with your comments on the changes you see around you. Suddenly you may discover a hidden delight in finding the hardest crossword puzzle imaginable, and solving it without any help from anyone else.

Growing old gracefully is a time for you to enjoy yourself, just being you.

HOW TO GET IN TOUCH
WITH THE INNER YOU

At the beginning of this book I suggested that one way to learn more about your Inner Self is to think of it as a little child, and as a

Virgo you should maybe think of it as a little child who needs to believe even more in him or her self. By learning to praise more than criticise, you will appreciate yourself a whole lot more too!

In order to do this, your own particular form of meditation can be very helpful as it will help you to still that busy mind and stop those worries slipping in, so that you can flow with what life has to offer.

The Virgo Meditation

Choose a quiet place so that no one can disturb you. Sit comfortably on the floor, in a cross legged position (or, if this is not comfortable, on a chair), close your eyes and visualise yourself sitting in front of the most beautiful painting you have ever seen. It is a painting of simple scenes of daily life, but so beautiful that you have nothing critical or negative to think about it. If thoughts come into your mind, let them slip by without worrying about them. Let yourself sink slowly into a meditative state for approximately twenty minutes, at the end of which you will be basking in the feeling of peace you have gained from this scene which then slowly starts to fade from your mind.

Try to do this twice a day. You will soon start to discover that your attitude to life can change, for you will always be able to remember the picture you have seen and will no longer feel the need to criticise or worry about every little thing. And don't worry that you won't know when the twenty minutes are up, for soon this will happen instinctively.

You may already have your own meditation technique and prefer to use that instead. All that's important is that you do it and recognise the benefits it can bring.

Then when you are washing and brushing your teeth each morning, look at yourself in the mirror and affirm to yourself with feeling and conviction:

I will not worry for the eternal light within me will protect me from harm

The more you understand your Inner Self, the easier it will be for you to realise that your worrying days really can be over, and that your analytical and discriminative powers can be put to more positive use when you have greater faith in *you*.

Your Personal Guide To The Future

By following the advice offered in this chapter you will understand and know yourself much better, and once you do that you will be able to have even more fulfilling relationships in your emotional and your working life. And you will be able to cope better in these fast moving times of change. It's not that you're suddenly going to change overnight and become an untidy slob instead of a perfectionist, or totally irresponsible in times of crisis. But you won't continually worry about whether you're doing the right thing or not, and you will feel much more inclined to let other people get on with their own thing if that's what they want, without feeling the need to pass on your critical views.

Perhaps your interest in health can lead you to be of service in the ever-increasing battle with Aids and drug abuse. You may discover you have a talent for counselling, or at very least helping to organise benefits or making youngsters more aware of the problems to be faced.

You will have learnt to expand your vision to the extent that you don't try to change the things you cannot change – but you'll certainly try to change those ones you can. And you'll even have learnt to laugh at yourself for worrying about tomorrow before it comes along!

You will have discovered that when you've learnt more about your Inner Self it will enable you to learn more about other people's deepest feelings too. Being balanced in your mind, body and soul means that even if crisis and chaos are more prevalent these days, your own outlook will remain positive and you will be able to achieve a whole lot more to help others too.

Positive Outlooks

★ Seeing perfection in what you already have
★ Learning to truly relax
★ Being bright, witty and sociable
★ Enjoying romance to the full
★ Living life more freely
★ Viewing tomorrow's world with more faith
★ Recognising your wonderful inherent good taste

Possible Pitfalls

★ Magnifying your faults
★ 'Nit-picking' too much
★ Putting work before *everything*
★ *Still* having no time for love
★ Being over-cautious
★ Seeing only dark clouds ahead
★ Trying to impose your standards on everyone else

For the typical Virgo, looking within can be something you prefer to avoid for fear of discovering things about yourself which need even more criticism. Forget all that! By getting to understand and know the Inner You there is no need to worry any more. Your own special voyage of self-discovery will enable you to deal calmly and collectedly with any turbulence you encounter in these changing times, and you will feel infinitely more fulfilled at the same time.

Libra

☆

SEPTEMBER 22 – OCTOBER 22

Libra is the seventh sign of the Zodiac, the sign of balance and harmony, and relates to marriage and partnership. You are a Masculine, Cardinal, Positive sign, the second of the Air signs, with Venus, Goddess of Love, as your planetary ruler. Symbolised by the Scales, you are the only sign to have an inanimate object as your symbol.

A charming, tactful, diplomatic, artistic, kind, generous, sociable human being – that's you. You generally possess a deep desire to make other people happy, and you endeavour to see beauty wherever possible in the world around you. Your sense of balance and fair play, your impeccable good taste and your bright and witty personality can make you a pleasure to be with; as do your sensitive, sentimental and softly sensual ways, especially when you're in love! Brigitte Bardot, Julie Andrews, Roger Moore, Julio Iglesias and Luke Perry were all born under your sign.

Peace and harmony at all costs are perhaps your deepest desires, and they might sound wonderful in theory. The only snag is that because of them you can be indecisive to the point of burying your head ostrich-like in the sand when you don't want to face up to something unpleasant, or by giving in on something which deep down you are against, particularly when you are involved in a relationship.

Libra is the first sign of the Autumn (Fall) and whereas your opposite sign of Aries has all the fiery enthusiasm brought on by the beginning of Spring you tend to stand back and contemplate – sometimes a little too long – before you decide to set your ideas and plans in motion. Procrastination is perhaps the greatest of your faults, and I've often felt that it's your own personal little safety-valve which in its own way stops you from looking too deep inside yourself for fear you don't like what you see!

Obviously, in any astrology book one can only generalise, and perhaps your own personal horoscope contains so many diverse planetary aspects that your Libra personality is overshadowed. But that is only speculation, and meanwhile it's time for you to learn how to balance your Libran scales so that the positives and negatives don't seem poles apart.

Meanwhile, I've often found that while Librans can appear to be such sweetness and light on the surface there is also a side of you which can simply cut off quite ruthlessly if you feel you're upsetting your own equilibrium, your inner need for balance and harmony, by becoming too involved in something you don't feel good about or someone who seems determined to upset you. And this has nothing to do with procrastination at all. It's simply that you are a whole lot stronger within than you appear to be on the surface. In lots of ways this is very positive, and it should therefore mean that it is basically very easy for you to keep those scales evenly balanced. However, so many of you tend to think that you don't actually cope terribly well unless you have someone who helps you do that balancing act, without realising that you have the most important person there all the time.

All of us have an outer personality and an inner one. In your particular case, learning to truly understand the Inner You will enable you to have greater clarity of vision regarding the Outer You, that person who tends to be so charming and affable to the world in general yet is sometimes having some kind of battle within, trying to find your own inner harmony. We all have something of our opposite sign within our own sign, and there is a lesson to be learnt from this. Your battles are not fought like

Aries, the Ram, but they are sometimes no less dramatic and exhausting! If you learn to fight your inner battles, you're going to face the outer world with a whole lot more confidence.

Later in this chapter you will find your very own meditation technique and affirmation to help you, but meanwhile it will certainly help for you to think of your inner personality rather like a little child. Since you invariably have a special affinity with children this could be easy for you to do. And the influence of Venus, Goddess of Love, which you share with Taurus as your planetary ruler means that you genuinely want to be loving and kind.

I'm not asking you to suddenly change your personality over-night, for that would almost certainly bring on one of the most enormous bouts of indecision you've ever known. But if you get to know your Inner Self better you will be able to trust your intuition more – and that is sure to mean that decision making doesn't have to be the agonising situation it can be for a lot of the Librans I've known personally, and I'm sure a whole lot more too.

You are invariably one of those highly intelligent people who need to communicate openly with other people. Barbara Walters, Johnny Carson, Anna Ford and Angela Rippon – all Librans! You're an Air sign like Gemini, but Gemini is far more restless than you who are often trying so hard to live on an even keel and end up feeling confused. But since you are so logical and always try to see both sides of the coin you will be among the first to realise and admit that the times we live in are becoming so chaotic and changing so fast that we need to find something else within ourselves in order to cope. Unfortunately, even the most highly evolved Librans cannot bring peace and harmony to the world without everyone else joining in and doing their bit. But when you achieve sufficient peace and harmony within your own person-ality it will be much easier to project it on others.

Burying heads in the sand just doesn't work any more. We're almost at the end of a millennium with massacres, Aids, drug wars, famine, environmental disasters and Mafia corruption becoming headline news almost every day, which makes it all the more vital to use your positive qualities to the full. I once wrote that Librans should perhaps write down the motto 'Procrastina-tion is the root of all evil' and remember it each day. Sadly, there are always evils of one kind or another, but when you create the right balance between your outer and inner personality you'll feel in a much stronger position to follow your own particular ideals.

Often when you feel yourself cutting off from dealing with something important, or realise that you simply cannot be bothered to listen to your friend's problems one minute more because they are really getting to you, it can also simply mean that you are out of tune with your own inner being. You need to calm yourself down, to become more tranquil yourself, as otherwise it can be very hard for you to live up to what others expect of you.

Positive and Negative, Yin and Yang, we need to have both. Once you begin to feel the balance between the Outer and the Inner You life in the 1990s will take on a different perspective, for you will have a deep-rooted belief in the decisions you make. Your intuition will become an integral part of your personality and you won't need to feel that you're not complete on your own.

PATHWAYS TO SUCCESS IN THE 1990s

★ Remember that harmony at any price doesn't mean cutting off from the world.
★ Accept that inner harmony truly does lead the way to balancing your Libran scales.
★ Create your very own calm centre without any help from your friends. You'll soon see it show outwardly.
★ Continue to see both sides of every situation, but listen to what your own inner voice tells you at the end and follow that.
★ Don't upset yourself if you can't always see perfection in everything – but keep on seeing the best there is.
★ Always remember that your opposite sign of Aries helps to give you inner strength too.

YOUR RULING PLANET . . .
Venus, Goddess of Love

One of the major influences on a male or female Libran is your planetary ruler. Venus, which rules your sign in addition to that of

Taurus, endows you with your love of beauty, peace and harmony, a love of love itself, and a love of colour, light and serenity. When Venus is your ruling planet, or indeed is strongly aspected in anyone's horoscope, there is almost always a strong attraction to and talent in art and music. Venus enables you to smile sweetly at the world, to love and be loved, and also helps to cushion the blows when hurts and disappointments come your way. Venus for you also seems to enhance your body in a very special way: so many of you have dimples somewhere – an extra booster to your charm!

However, it's best to warn you that there is a tendency for some of you to think that being in a perfect relationship is the be-all and end-all of life itself. Watch out that you continue to concentrate on learning to live with and love *you* inwardly, balancing your *own* scales, before you go on in the same old way expecting Prince or Princess Charming to balance them for you.

In the body Venus rules the throat, thymus gland and kidneys. Venus is also the chief planet of the Heart Chakra, with her quiet beauty creating a special sanctuary within your heart.

Venus rises in the sky before the Sun as the Morning Star. The Central American Indians believed this related to her reincarnation and that when she reappears again as the Evening Star it means she has been through her earthly trials and tribulations and is ready to leave again.

Some modern interpretations of classical mythology have tended to portray Venus far more as a sex goddess than as the goddess of love, but the Romans associated Venus with nature and beauty and the Greeks with Aphrodite, their own Goddess of love. Modern Goddess lore tends to link Aphrodite with someone who definitely prefers to be in a relationship rather than on their own – which is very much the Libran personality.

Every Zodiac sign has its own particular colour or colours, and blues, especially pale blue, and pinks tend to be associated with Libra (as they are with Taurus).

Your planetary symbol is the Scales, and justice and harmony are extremely important to Libra. Around 2000 BC the Libra constellation was linked by the Babylonians to the judging of the living and the dead, and the ancient Egyptians used the time of the Full Moon in Libra to weigh their harvest. Libra was called the Astrological Lady of the Scales after Libera, the Goddess whom the Carthaginians worshipped as Astroarche, Queen of the Stars. She has always represented the balancing process of karmic law, so it is so important for you to apply that balancing process to your own inner and outer life. The Roman Venus-Aphrodite related to matriarchal justice and natural law – again very much the traits of your sign. The Goddess of Justice in those ancient days supposedly held the scales of everyone's fate, and was not blindfolded as she is now depicted. Libra represents the Autumn (Fall) Equinox, when night and day are equal.

As a Libran, with Venus as your ruler and the Scales as your symbol, you really do have so much going for you if you can learn to balance your caring, loving ways and sense of fair play and justice with greater sense of your own potential and ability to be a star in your own right without the need for reassurance from anyone else.

THE INNER CHALLENGE – THE OUTER CHANGE

There are sure to be some areas of your life which don't always work out exactly as you would like, or times when you have realised that by taking so long to make up your mind about something special an opportunity has slipped by and you have lost out on something which might have been just right for you.

But Librans aren't usually soft and pliable people, unable to stick up for what you believe in. When you know exactly what it is you want, you won't give in. Sting is a good example of someone who has recognised what is happening to the world and is trying hard to help with the preservation of the Rain Forests; and Martina Navratilova refused to allow her age to make her consider leaving championship tennis.

The following areas will all be important to you in one way or another, and if you're prepared to leave 'procrastination' and 'vacillation' out of your vocabulary and resolve to listen to what your inner voice has to tell you, your Libran scales could end up balanced in the most perfect way.

RELATIONSHIPS

If there is one sign who truly doesn't want to be alone it's invariably a Libran. Of course it's all down to your feeling that you simply aren't complete if you're not in a partnership. And this can sometimes lead you into disastrous relationships which deep down you know are going nowhere but at least they mean you have someone in your life. Rather like Leo, you're in love with love; but whereas Leo remains dominant and forceful, your mind tends to convince you that being without someone to love is not something you particularly care to contemplate.

Deep down you sometimes wish you were as devil-may-care as your opposite sign of Aries, or had Leo's enormous ego, but I'm afraid to say that you can be rather self-indulgent and convince yourself that you really do need a relationship in order to feel whole. There's something naive and immature about this side of your nature. The wonderful thing about opening yourself up to your Inner Voice is that you will discover that your deepest needs also relate to being in tune with yourself, and not totally to being in tune with someone else – no matter how wonderful that can be when the relationship is properly balanced.

The guide opposite will help you to see the benefits of getting to know the Inner You when romance is involved!

By delving deeper into your inner being you really will start to appreciate yourself for who you truly are. Once you learn to admit that you can take care of your own needs it's going to be a whole lot easier to have balanced relationships with everyone else in your life and with those who are still to come your way.

You will see that a romantic relationship, when it is properly balanced, can give both you and your partner infinite satisfaction on all levels. And if there isn't anyone in your life at the moment, don't worry about it. Enjoy having a relationship with that special person who is you!

The Outer You   sees Aries as far too impulsive and headstrong; wonders if Taurus could be a decision maker for you; enjoys intellectual chats with Gemini but doubts Gemini will settle down: is not too keen on Cancer's moodiness in your life; could easily be flattered and charmed by Leo; fears that Virgo will analyse what you'd rather hide; wonders if all Librans are indecisive like you; the thought of the sex symbol of the Zodiac almost sends you running from Scorpio; can't see happy-go-lucky Sagittarius wanting a permanent relationship; fears that Capricorn's materialistic ways may preclude very much romance; sees Aquarius as another sign who wants to be free and easy far too much; recognises that there can be lots of romance with Pisces but worries about more material things.

The Inner You   realises that the challenges presented by your opposite sign of Aries could be incredibly positive; with Taurus senses what bliss two Venus ruled signs can have together; feels that mental stimulation with Gemini can often lead to love; thinks about your own need to balance yourself and understands Cancer's fluctuating moods a little better; loves being in love with Leo and enjoys being praised to the hilt yourself; you know you're a perfectionist yourself – so at least you should understand Virgo deep down; with Libra you could have the perfect balancing act if you both resolve to understand each other's inner personality too; doesn't fear Scorpio's passionate ways and has greater belief in yourself; enjoys being with Sagittarius for the fun you have together and lets tomorrow take care of itself; at least knows that Capricorn will really work hard at a good relationship, so gives it a chance; doesn't worry quite so much if Aquarius doesn't always tell you how much you're cared for; with Pisces, doesn't spend too much valuable time gazing at each other with adoring looks!

CAREERS AND BUSINESS

Both male and female Librans often seem to be unfairly described not only as indecisive but also lazy. I can vouch for this being unfair from among the Librans I know myself. Those who work manage to put in long hours at their place of work and don't leave things unfinished at home either. What is true yet again of course, is that you have problems with decision making. But once you have learnt to balance your outer and inner personalities, by having faith not simply in your intuition but also in what you're capable of, the 'lazy' description could start to disappear from astrology books and columns!

It's more important than ever these days to make sure you do everything possible to safeguard your job, and sometimes decisions will not necessarily be left to you anyway. There is more and more unemployment, companies and factories are closing down all over the world, and therefore you can't afford to take any risks for yourself.

Even so, no matter how brilliantly you manage to balance your Libran Scales you will probably always prefer to work in the company of other people rather than completely on your own. And that is fine too, as long as you don't subjugate your own personality in so doing and miss out on chances to fulfil your own ambitions. For never forget it, you are born with a great deal of ambition – it's just that you're sometimes afraid to 'go for the big one' in case it slips out of your grasp.

Stop battling with your Inner Self, Libra! Look at yourself inwardly and recognise both your talents *and* your limitations – we all have to have some of those!

Many of you possess great artistic talent, and while you're not all going to end up as poets, painters or musicians (John Lennon was one of the most famous musicians of our time), your sense of beauty and aesthetic eye often draw you in some way to the arts. So don't allow a lack of confidence make you doubt your abilities. You make excellent art dealers, interior designers, judges, law-yers, diplomats, counsellors, beauty specialists, hairdressers, per-sonnel managers and stewards and stewardesses, and are often marvellous working in PR, advertising, the world of fashion (Ralph Lauren is a Libran) or the entertainment industry. Successful Librans include Gore Vidal, Margaret Thatcher, Arthur Miller, Luciano Pavarotti, Bruce Springsteen and Sir Georg Solti.

How Do You Handle Decisions?

No, I'm really not joking. I've already gone on about your indecisive ways earlier in this chapter so I'm not going to go too much into that now except to say that the way you have handled decisions in the past has almost certainly been by weighing up the pros and cons of a given situation and probably taking far too long to come up with the answer.

There will always be decisions of one kind or another to be made in life. Somehow the more we encounter chaos around us in this changing world, the more decisions related to our personal lives, our professional situation or our children seem to suddenly be sprung upon us. Things move at a much faster pace nowadays. You can't get away with writing a letter in reply – a fax has to be sent, which is immediate and gives you even less time to ponder! So really you have no choice but to trust your inner voice and to become so much in tune with your inner being that you will instinctively know what is best for you. There are lots of Librans who don't hesitate when it comes to making decisions. Margaret Thatcher was one of them. So it doesn't mean that you are *all* bad at this, though some of you definitely are!

Always remember too that with something of your opposite sign of Aries inside your own personality you're a whole lot stronger than you think. And while you may have become used to passing the decision making to someone else in your life, you really do have the ability to be responsible for yourself. It can be a whole lot of fun too!

How Do You Handle Conflicts?

It's fairly obvious that once your attitude to decision making begins to change you will be able to deal with conflicts in an easier way too.

Actually, conflicts are often something you excel at dealing with if you're on the outside looking in. Since you hate arguments of any kind you usually try desperately hard not to involve yourself in anything which could raise your voice or your blood pressure. The impulsiveness of your opposite sign of Aries might horrify you, and nit-picking Virgo might drive you wild, but you will cope. However, cruelty of any kind to man or beast will certainly have you joining in of your own free will, and Brigitte Bardot and Sting are of course two Librans who personify this characteristic. One of my own best friends will never turn away a homeless cat.

You have an inborn ability to see both sides of any disagreement, and if the conflict does involve you there is sometimes a tendency for you to give in simply because you hate the thought of arguing any more. That is fine if you feel the other person is in the right, but it's going to show your weakness if you really do have right on your side. Sometimes people tend to say that Librans simply don't have a competitive spirit – but what about Martina Navratilova?

It's certainly true that you hate disharmony of any kind. It definitely creates a conflict between the Inner and the Outer You. You also don't like ugliness, but then not many people do.

There is the conflict within you that you're not a complete person without the perfect partner. In his last years the multi-talented John Lennon seemed to feel he simply couldn't deal with life without Yoko Ono by his side at all times. But understanding your Inner Self, accepting that you are a complete person just as you are, will make it a whole lot easier for you to accept conflicts as just episodes in life which come and go – and don't often have to be a major issue in your life.

You As A Parent

A Libran parent ought to be one of the most caring and lovable parents in the whole wide world. You're so kind, affectionate and sweet that Libran Julie Andrews simply had to be the perfect choice for Maria in 'The Sound of Music'.

However, there can be a tendency for some of you to look on your partner as the sole entity in your life, and children tend to come second instead of forming part of a family unit. One parent families may sometimes find it hard bringing up children for this reason, and that is why becoming stronger through being at one with your Inner Self and knowing your own capabilities will enable you to have a more happily balanced family relationship. You will invariably be a fair-minded and easy-going parent, teaching your offspring the difference between right and wrong, explaining how justice works and all about the problems which are created by promiscuity and drugs. And you are sure to instil in them your own inherent good taste wherever possible. There is a sweetness and a loving quality given to you by your ruling planet Venus which is often noticed by children of other families – and indeed you do try hard to do the best you can.

COPING WITH LIFE AFTER BREAK-UPS OR BEREAVEMENTS

It's often easier for you to cope with a bereavement than a break-up if the bereavement was an inevitable fact of nature, for your ability to see situations clearly is a great asset. With a break-up, especially if it was not of your volition, it is often very hard for you to accept that you have to cope with life on your own again.

However, both situations can pose big problems for those of you who have never bothered to listen to your inner voice in order to learn more about yourself as a separate entity and someone who could function perfectly well without a partner. I've noticed that Librans seem to re-marry or settle with a new person more quickly than other signs, especially Libran men. It's that fear of being alone rising up, the feeling that you need another person to bring you balance. But once you've learnt to become balanced with *you*, you will be able to cope with things in a much more philosophical way and get on with your own life without the desperate need to try immediately to replace what you have lost.

LIFESTYLE, HEALTH AND DIET

The Libra lifestyle is preferably one which embodies the good things of life. With your Venus ruler, you can be as sybaritic as any Taurean and as luxury loving as Leo; quite happy to play in the fast lane as long as you have plenty of time to laze around, soak up the sun or simply sleep late into the day. Exercise doesn't always figure as one of your greatest joys, although having said that I must mention Navratilova yet again and also Imran Khan. Often you'd rather sit there on the sidelines having a long cool drink and watch someone else doing all the energetic stuff.

However, since you are dedicated to the body beautiful and towards looking youthful for as long as you can (why *is* it that even when you do start to grow old you have such a magical way of looking years younger than the rest of us?), you're a natural for saunas and massages, aromatherapy, reflexology and all the other things which help to make you feel and look wonderful. It was a Libran, Joseph Corvo, who became an expert in Zone Therapy, another form of pressure point massage on the feet and hands which I can personally vouch for as being an incredible bonus to one's health.

In order to become more in touch with your Inner Self, to find that inner peace which is so important, Yoga is one of the best activities you could do. It will help to balance your mind, body and spirit in the purest way possible and ensure that you feel supple and youthful throughout your life. There is no age limit to Yoga, and its benefits are truly endless.

With your interest in the arts you usually like to see as many exhibitions, concerts, plays and films as your schedule will allow. Get-togethers with friends are also a very pleasurable way of filling your time although you can be somewhat lazy about doing much of the arranging yourself. Basically you like to relax! Social occasions are wonderful as long as you don't have to mix with stressful people who upset your equilibrium, for while you're quite brilliant at smiling brilliantly and saying all the right things even to people for whom you don't care, inwardly you will feel very different.

I'm sorry to tell you this but your eating habits can be fairly unbalanced as you have a tendency to over-indulge yourself with rich foods and too much good wine. That's fine once in a while, Libra, but if you start to make too much of a habit of it you're going to be asking for trouble. I think Luciano Pavarotti must be an exception! There's a tendency for you to like sweet things just a little bit too much, and you need to watch out that your silhouette doesn't start to suffer. Think of the trouble the Duchess of York went to in order to try to keep in shape! But crash diets are never the answer. Learn to plan your dietary regime with a little more thoroughness and keep your body in trim.

Libra rules the bladder and kidneys, which are responsible for regulating the liquid in the body and for eliminating waste. Both react to inner stress and over-indulgence – all the more reason to appreciate tranquillity as well as keeping a careful eye on your diet and the amount that you drink so as not to upset your health through self-abuse! Libra also rules your nervous system so problems can develop if you're not prepared to be true to yourself over your relationships and the emotional pattern of your life. Keeping your equilibrium balanced inwardly and outwardly is equally important to avoid the threat of ulcers which often seem to prevail among Librans, especially those who feel less than harmonious deep within.

Meditation will be especially good for you as an aid to calming your mind if you feel all the pressures of the world closing in upon you, and a special technique for you will be given a little further on in this chapter.

GROWING OLD GRACEFULLY

The beautiful thing about growing old for you is that you will rarely show your true age. One of my closest family is eighty-nine years old and looks remarkable. When she was already almost eighty she flew for the very first time to visit me in Milan where I was then living and everyone remarked upon her perfect, unlined English rose complexion. So at least you don't have to worry about your looks!

Of course, it's back to the same old thing and to how self-sufficient you have become if you have to grow old gracefully on your own. But if you're in tune with your higher self, that Inner You, you're never really alone anyway.

Look on the benefits of having time on your hands to do all the things you always wanted to do. Since you care about being with people, why not volunteer to do some charity work at your local hospital or elsewhere? Help is needed more and more. And always remember not to turn on the news reports late at night. It's never a good thing to see bad news just before you go to sleep – it upsets the equilibrium, which is just what a Libran doesn't need!

Growing old gracefully is a time for you to enjoy yourself, with other people around or just being you.

How To Get In Touch With The Inner You

At the beginning of this book I suggested that one way to learn more about your Inner Self is to think of it as a little child, and as a Libran you could perhaps think of it as a little child who needs to realise that he or she is a real person all by him or herself. By this means you will also really appreciate the strength and potential of your outer persona.

In order to do this your own particular form of meditation (see opposite) can be very helpful. It will help you to calm down and overcome any emotional imbalance so that you can flow with what life has to offer you.

Of course, you may have your own way of meditating already. That doesn't matter, for the important thing is that you recognise the benefits which regular meditation can bring you.

Then each morning when you are washing and brushing your teeth, look at yourself in the mirror and affirm to yourself with feeling and conviction:

I am ready to merge my outer personality
with my inner self to achieve greater balance

The more you understand your Inner Self, the easier it will be for you to realise that decisions don't have to be the hassle of all time. Being at ease with yourself in all situations will enable you to go forward to the 21st century with a more confident and positive outlook.

☆──☆

The Libra Meditation

Choose a quiet place so that no one can disturb you. Sit comfortably on the floor, in a cross legged position (or, if this is not comfortable, on a chair), close your eyes and visualise a beautiful golden set of scales standing in front of you with one side higher for a moment and then the other. Allow your mind to be still, but don't worry if thoughts do keep coming in; just let them drift by, for all you are concerned with are the beautiful scales and watching them gradually, gradually reach a perfect balance – the sides level with each other. Let yourself sink into a meditative state for approximately twenty minutes. Don't worry if one side of the scales becomes a little higher: simply visualise it balancing out again and always leave it balanced perfectly before you start to slowly open your eyes at the end of the twenty minutes.

You will soon start to discover that making decisions and living a more balanced life in the real world become easier. And don't worry, you will begin to know instinctively when the twenty minutes are up.

☆──☆

YOUR PERSONAL GUIDE TO THE FUTURE

By following the advice offered in this chapter you will come to understand and know yourself much better. And once you do that you will be able to have even more fulfilling relationships in your emotional and working life and thus be able to cope better in the ever-changing times in which we live.

It's not that you will suddenly change overnight and become an impulsive Aries instead of a slow decision maker, or that you will never again feel the need for approval. But those things won't happen quite so often and gradually you will find that your Libran scales no longer need someone else to balance them.

You may find that your interest in communication inspires you to join a group of like-minded people who are together for a common purpose, whether it be Greenpeace, saving the Rain Forests, one of the humanitarian aid organisations or a drug or Aids advice group. You will have learnt the difference between relaxation and simply being lazy, about trusting your inner voice and your own mind, and will be able to give more to other people when you have made self-acceptance your personal trademark.

When you are truly balanced in mind, body and soul you will understand and appreciate other people's innermost feelings more too. And in these days when tragedies of one kind or another really do seem to hit the headlines with ever-increasing regularity you could often find yourself called upon by relatives or neighbours to provide a calming influence and the warmth and compassion which is so much a part of your personality.

Positive Outlooks

★ Discovering your true potential
★ Relying on your own judgement
★ Retaining your own identity
★ Being a real peace-maker
★ Balancing those scales at last
★ Having a great relationship with you
★ Enjoying what comes next

Possible Pitfalls

★ Giving in to insecurity
★ Still taking too long to decide
★ Searching too much for a partner
★ Sitting too often on the fence
★ Giving in to imbalance again
★ Not loving yourself enough
★ Not living in the now

For the typical Libra looking within may be something you'd rather put off until another day, wondering whether you will like what you discover. But don't do that! By getting to know and accept the Inner You, you will find it so much easier to find the peace and harmony you yearn for. Don't put it off any longer. You won't regret it.

Scorpio

— ☆ —

OCTOBER 23 – NOVEMBER 21

Scorpio is the eighth sign of the Zodiac. It relates to death and rebirth and also to joint financial issues, investments and inheritances. You are a Feminine, Fixed, Negative sign, the second of the Water signs. Both Mars, God of War, and Pluto, Lord of the Underworld, are your planetary rulers, and your planetary symbol is the Scorpion. The Serpent and Eagle are also linked symbolically with you. You're the only Fixed (i.e. immovable) Water sign, and as such need to be careful that the emotional tendency of Water doesn't become either static or stagnant.

A magnetic, charismatic, profound, perceptive, intuitive to the point of being extremely psychic personality who is passionately emotional, highly creative, persistent, intense and courageous, that's you – and even that is probably an understatement. You have a charisma unlike any of the other Zodiac signs (think of Vivien Leigh and Richard Burton), and it's also true that you are one of those invincible human beings who can rise above all odds, just like a Phoenix rising from the ashes.

However, when your emotions are frustrated it can be all too easy for you to become secretive and highly suspicious, intense and introverted, jealous and broodingly resentful. And there is an incredibly self-destructive and troubled side to your nature which can come to the surface. Charles Manson is always being used as an example of the dark side of the Scorpio nature for the simple reason that he personified this in the most obvious of ways. It's not just Virgo who can be obsessive and compulsive where details are concerned. When you're in one of your self-destructive moods you are feeling things intensely deeply, and there is an egoistic side to your nature which makes it hard for you to let go when you decide that you deeply want something or someone.

Obviously, in any astrology book one can only generalise, and perhaps your own personal horoscope contains so many diverse planetary aspects that your Scorpio personality is overshadowed and nobody would guess you were a Scorpio. But that is pure conjecture, and meanwhile we want to get people away from that 'sting in the Scorpion's tail' idea which always seems to come up when you're around.

Once you realise that it is in your power not to have to worry about people backing away from you at parties when you mention you're a Scorpio, life will be a whole lot easier. The world around us has been changing so much that old ways no longer prevail, so why not make the best possible use of your regenerative powers? If you feel you've been living too much on a lower Scorpio level it's time to realise that you can start to soar like the eagle which is the more evolved Scorpio personality. Of course, you can always stick somewhere in the middle and be that Scorpio snake or serpent – but if you aim for the top it will be much more rewarding, not just inwardly but outwardly too.

Think of how lucky you are! You're blessed with two planetary rulers, Mars and Pluto, who give you your fighting spirit, energy and invincibility and the ability to transform your life when you really choose to do so.

We all have an outer personality and an inner one. In your case, discovering and learning to understand the Inner You can be quite a mind-blowing experience! You're already used to creeping into your own private little space, but you don't necessarily look around and see what is there. Later in this chapter you will find your own meditation technique and affirmation to help you relax and go within in a calm and relaxed way. Meanwhile, some of you with your finely tuned intuition may even decide to think of your inner personality as the dark side of your character, or perhaps your shadow, the part you prefer to keep hidden from the rest of the world. Getting to know and understand the reason for this dark side can be one of the best lessons you've ever learnt, for it will enable you to have a better relationship not just with yourself but with everyone else you deal with too.

Scorpio is renowned as the 'sex symbol of the Zodiac', and you're certainly not shy about putting forward your claims in this department! Your ego is amazingly large; in fact you could even make quite a few Leos seem meek and mild in comparison – though that *would* take some doing. However, the sexual side of your personality, if unexpressed or thwarted in a way which leaves you feeling emotionally unfulfilled (for you are often an idealistic romantic too), can lead the dark side of your nature to express itself in a far more unhealthy way, leading to a greater interest in promiscuity and pornography and so often to a deep inner loneliness.

It is also fairly obvious that if a Scorpio who is continually determined to prove his or her sexual prowess does not take extra care then problems could be in store because of the ever-increasing Aids situation as well as other sexually transmitted diseases. Happily, on the positive side there is also an increasing interest in personal growth and spirituality, giving you every reason to learn about the needs of your Inner Self and to discover that sexual gratification alone doesn't make up for a true mind-body-soul involvement. And you can use your sexuality in a different way – a way to transform yourself into a higher state of consciousness. (In Eastern philosophy this relates to the Kundalini energy which lies like a snake at the bottom of the spine.)

Amazingly enough, there is often such a deep insecurity lurking beneath the surface of your charismatic outer being that you feel you can't live without an intensely emotional love affair – which sometimes ends up being almost a compulsive obsession. Your self-advertised need for privacy is often to cover up those moments when you actually feel very alone but would hate anyone to know it.

It may seem strange to anyone other than a Scorpio to read that what you often need more than anything else is to believe in yourself as someone who is deeply loyal, genuinely interested in religion, reform and healing, and someone who can be one of the most protective and affectionate people in the Zodiac.

Creating the right balance between your inner and your outer personality isn't always easy, and it isn't something that can be achieved overnight. But if you will stop frustrating yourself by yearning intensely for the things which perhaps are not meant to be yours and will start to use your tremendous inner strength to let you see the joys that life still has to offer – perhaps by living one day at a time – then you will be doing yourself the best service in the world!

Any time you feel you're getting into one of your heavy, brooding moods because you're feeling frustrated and held back, start to think about your opposite sign of Taurus. We all have something of our opposite signs within us and they can teach us something too. Taurus knows the world cannot be changed overnight and has the patience to work slowly but surely on what needs to be done. Your invincibility, plus a little extra patience and lots of positive input, can work wonders for you.

We all have Positive and Negative, Yin and Yang within us. Once you truly know how to balance your outer and inner personalities your life will become more rewarding for you will have learnt how to expand your vision and not to give in to the dark feelings which held you back in the past.

PATHWAYS TO SUCCESS IN THE 1990S

★ Be that soaring eagle rising high in the heavens . . . not the scorpion who in a self-destructive way stings himself to death when surrounded by a ring of fire.

★ Direct your passionate emotions to something other than your own sexual gratification.

★ Try to let your ego take second place to your heart!

★ Vow to become more conscious of yourself as a valuable human being.

★ Stop hanging on to the past and to past fears or rejections – expand your vision to try to see the good things in life.

★ Resolve to try to eradicate possessiveness and jealousy from your life – or be more willing to understand when it's used upon you!

YOUR RULING PLANETS . . . Mars, God of War, and Pluto, Lord of the Underworld

Among the major influences on a male or female Scorpio are your planetary rulers. Since Mars, who also rules Aries, was the Roman God of War, it is perhaps no wonder that you are considered invincible, ready to fight to the end and die for your deep-felt beliefs. You can read more about Mars on pages 9–10 in the Aries chapter, for it is important also to tell you about Pluto here.

Pluto as a planet was only discovered in 1930. In classical mythology another name for Pluto was Hades, who ruled the Underworld with Persephone. In Christian times he was also supposed to represent the Devil. But Pluto's astrological associations are with the regenerative and creative force of the body, and Pluto relates to the underworld of volcanoes and earthquakes, to enforced change and to the beginnings and endings of life phases – perhaps leading to the interest of so many Scorpios in the occult, religion, and reincarnation.

With Mars *and* Pluto ruling your sign it's not surprising that you have such great inner strength and such powers of regeneration. It's simply a question of getting them into the right balance, which is why understanding the Inner You will be such a help.

Every sign has its own particular colour or colours, and deep crimson is the one usually identified with Scorpio. Magenta or a sort of reddish-violet is also associated with Pluto and relates to purification of the blood and the stimulation of higher sexual energy.

Your planetary symbol is invariably known as the Scorpion, and this is the symbol usually taken to illustrate you. But there is also the Serpent or Snake, and more especially the Eagle which represents your powerful ability to transcend the difficulties of the world and achieve your highest potential. The Scorpion, Snake and Eagle are all related to life and death. The ancient Egyptians knew the constellation Scorpio as Selquet, who was the Goddess responsible for freeing hordes of scorpions during Egypt's yearly sandstorms, and they called its stars the 'serpent stars'. Ever since the Garden of Eden snakes have been symbolic both mystically and religiously, and their relationship to Scorpio is their shared ability to cast off their old skins and to create new ones, just as the Earth is renewed annually. And the Eagle has always symbolised regeneration.

As a Scorpio with all these mythological links to your sign you have immense powers to draw upon to lead you up onto a higher level which will enable you to make your mark upon the world in an extremely important way.

The Inner Challenge – The Outer Change

There are areas in the lives of all of us which do not work out just as we would like. But that doesn't mean you have to sink down to the depths of depression or press the self-destruct button.

If you think about it in a positive way you have more going for you than the rest of us – a natural inborn ability to transform your life, to be reborn without even having to leave the planet. Think about how you can help other people – it will stop you thinking about any problems of your own quite so much, and you will definitely be doing something constructive about them too. It's fascinating to me how many Scorpio people who did go down to the bottom in one way or another also managed to regenerate themselves in a way which enabled them to be of immense service to others. While writing this book I was fortunate enough to meet a very special Scorpio lady, a healer who had herself been cured of cancer which at the time (three years ago) was thought to be incurable. She is one of the brightest, most vital people you could meet, spending her time helping others as a very big thank you for being saved herself. Scorpio people often turn deeply to religion which they then have to pass on to others. Billy Graham is a perfect example of this.

It's so important for you to accept that we all have two sides to our personalities. When you come to terms with that inner one and transform its negative qualities into ones which vibrate at that higher level you will start to say goodbye to your fears and insecurities for good.

RELATIONSHIPS

Anyone who has ever had a relationship with a Scorpio will have to admit that you are *not* easy. Exciting, captivating, fascinating, exceptionally emotional and passionate – yes. But easy is not a word which could often be used to describe you. Perhaps one of the kindest words to use would be exhilarating, for you can certainly take someone to the heights of ecstasy – often all too easily!

The trouble with you is that because you are invariably so jealous and possessive there is the obsessive fear that you cannot live without the object of your affections. And yet often it is incredibly difficult for you to live with them. I've always thought that the love affair . . . marriage . . . love affair between Richard Burton and Elizabeth Taylor was one of the greatest love stories of our time. He was Scorpio and she is Pisces.

There is another side to you which is attracted to a chosen partner, whether for emotional, sexual, material or spiritual reasons, but which then seems to resent the very things which first attracted you and ends almost draining that partner of his or her greatest assets. It's almost as though you are sometimes caught up in a great psychological power game. The wonderful thing about listening to what your inner voice has to say is that you will realise that you tend to go to extremes in too many ways and that a proper balance of your mind, body and spirit can enable you to enjoy much happier and healthier relationships all round.

Use the guide (on page 130) to help you see the benefits of getting to know the Inner You when romance is involved.

By going deeper inside and learning what your deepest needs and desires really represent you will find it easier to recognise and respect what you need from a romantic relationship. You will discover that your sexual desires won't be inhibited in any way but that in addition you will realise how important it is for you to feel totally at one with another human being in a real mind, body and soul relationship.

Learning more about the Inner You will inspire you to learn more about the inner feelings of everyone who is important in your life so that all your relationships become even more rewarding and worthwhile.

The Outer You   sees Aries as equally power conscious and a sexual dynamo; finds the sensuality of your opposite sign of Taurus a definite turn-on; thinks Gemini talks far too much; finds Cancer's sentimentality too cloying; realises it's a battle of the egos to the end with Leo; somewhat resents Virgo's cool appraisal of your talents; wonders how to charm romantic Libra into a quick decision; who stings whom first? – that's the obvious question with Scorpio; all that Sagittarius optimism is good for you if you would only realise it; you're attracted to Capricorn's material success, but they may not be sexy enough for you; cool, detached and often unemotional Aquarius could frustrate any passionate desires; Pisces may be just too soft and pliable to cope with someone like you!

The Inner You   finds Aries sexually stimulating and loves all that energy; realises your opposite sign of Taurus can fulfil so many of your inner needs; accepts that you'll have to learn to open up a little more to get on with Gemini; understands that with Cancer sentimentality and sensitivity can make a sexual relationship far more profound; finds Leo almost as magnetic and charismatic as you consider yourself; understands that a little Virgo criticism could actually be good for you to take; is willing to take time to balance those Libran scales and find peace within too; sees that another Scorpio can help you to understand so much about your innermost needs; flies to the moon with Sagittarius but never tries to possess such a free spirit; resolves never to show jealousy when Capricorn is working late again; accepts that Aquarius is just as powerful as you, but in a much, much cooler way; both you and Pisces are pretty psychic, and there could sometimes be a soulmate relationship brewing.

CAREERS AND BUSINESS

Both male and female Scorpios are often powerhouses of energy when it comes to career and business issues. You will invariably strive courageously to reach the heights and your shrewd mind and instinct are at their best when used to get to the roots of any problems. You usually have a fantastic memory and great powers of concentration and you are certainly not afraid of either hard work or setbacks. You are also immensely loyal both as a boss and as an employee. But if your creative desires are blocked in any way there is a tendency for an almost ruthless obsession to take over, and that dark side of the Scorpio personality can come to the fore all too easily. There is also another interesting side to this in that the way you're feeling emotionally plays an extremely strong part in the way you cope with your work. Scorpio Julia Roberts was an example of this after her much publicised break-up with Kiefer Sutherland, but that invincible Scorpio strength always comes through in the end, and she is no less a star now than she was then! Other creative Scorpios include Whoopi Goldberg, Bryan Adams, Richard Dreyfuss, Calvin Klein, Katherine Hepburn and Natalia Makarova.

Your power complex can, when used in a negative way, turn you into a ruthless manipulative egocentric. It is therefore so important that you become in tune spiritually with your Inner Self and direct those negative thoughts into positive aspirations, for your potential is limitless. Your ability to analyse and research can perhaps be of great use in working for the good of humanity in these days of immense suffering throughout so many parts of the world. You *know* you can rise from defeats and setbacks to wherever you choose, and that is where your power truly lies.

Career-wise you can excel in many ways. You're often exceedingly good at finance, handling other people's money and business affairs, psychiatry, psychology, being a detective, orator, debater, pharmacist, medium, healer, lawyer, scientist (both Carl Sagan and Michel Gauquelin are Scorpios), psychic investigator, surgeon, religious minister (Billy Graham) and royalty (King Hussein of Jordan and Prince Charles).

You are invariably prepared to study long into the night to achieve something worthwhile professionally. And it's not unusual to find Scorpios taking degrees in their chosen subjects later in life.

Always let your inner voice be your best friend and remember that Eagle soaring to the heights, transcending all earthly problems. For sometimes those of you who haven't become as successful as you hoped tend to harbour resentment against the people who have, which is definitely *not* very positive!

Professionally, deep down you know you have the power to succeed. But let that success be something which brings you pleasure where you need it most, in that private part of your personality which is your Inner You. Just concentrate on being the best you can for *you*. Let the other people get on with what *they* have to do without feeling you always have to compete.

How Do You Handle Decisions?

There is no way you can get through life without having to make decisions at some time or another. And one of the great assets of being a Scorpio is that you are blessed with such wonderful sixth sense, perception, intuition, psychic ability – call it what you will – that you invariably know deep down what you need to do in almost any given situation. That is, of course, if you are properly in tune with your inner voice and prepared to follow its directions.

It's also important that you forget all about ego, possessiveness, jealousy, and all those other Scorpio characteristics and make your decisions purely on what each situation represents in itself. There really is no point getting yourself emotionally embroiled over every little thing which needs to be decided upon. Sometimes your decision may have to involve relinquishing power in some way, which is all the more reason to delve deep within to soul level and be honest to yourself as well as to everyone else.

If a particular decision involves changing your life in some way think of it as a blessing, for you thrive on transformation and must never forget that! Just remember that by balancing your inner feelings and your outer actions you will be on the right track.

How Do You Handle Conflicts?

I've often wondered if 'Hell hath no fury like a woman scorned' was intended for Scorpio – and not just in relation to women either! Conflicts never seem to be easy for so many of you. Either you bottle things up inside and shower the object of your anger with dark resentful looks and total silence; or you go into quite a violent rage.

Although you can be amazingly loyal and deeply emotional towards the people and issues you believe in, there is a conflict between the light and dark sides of your personality which seems never to be more apparent than in times of disagreement. I honestly don't think, it is true that Scorpios cannot forgive but I must admit that I think they find it incredibly hard to forget a slight, however small it may be.

Because you are a person of such extremes it will be extremely valuable when you allow your inner voice to show you how to release your emotional fears and insecurities and become much more positive about yourself. You will start to see conflicts most of the time as little more than annoyances that we all go through, and you will lose your obsessiveness about them.

When you feel someone is impinging on your privacy and turn on them in anger, why not smile to yourself as you realise that this is often just the sort of thing *you* do to others! So often the things which make us mad in other people are the things we don't like to admit about ourselves – perhaps remembering this could be valuable for you. Why stress yourself out worrying about your own personal conflicts? Put your powers of intuition into thinking up ways to help other people resolve *their* conflicts, for more and more people have personal problems in these unsettled times.

You As A Parent

You will usually be a very loving parent though you may have a tendency to be quite strict and dictatorial too. You certainly won't put up with any nonsense from your children when they are growing up and you will expect, and if necessary demand, their respect. But just because you are a Fixed sign it doesn't mean that you have to be fixed in your opinions and demands all the time.

You're not always the most light-hearted parent in the world but there is usually no doubt that you are very emotional about your offspring, even if you do tend to hide your feelings. Try to unwind a little bit and don't be quite so intense. In these days of growing crime, drug abuse and sexually transmitted diseases it is so important to be close to your children; to be someone they know they can come to and talk over their problems with freely without the fear that you will coldly turn a shoulder or tell them to never darken your door again. The lovely thing about you is your loyalty, and your children will know they can come to you even later in life if they have problems and don't know which way to turn.

COPING WITH LIFE AFTER BREAK-UPS OR BEREAVEMENTS

Although this doesn't necessarily relate to you personally, I thought it worthwhile to mention something which I read years ago in Linda Goodman's book *Sun Signs* and which always fascinated me. She had written that there is a strange astrological pattern which brings about the death of a family relative in either the year before or the year after a Scorpio is born. And when a Scorpio dies there is going to be a birth within the family also in the year before or after. She said that this happens at least ninety-five per cent of the time. The power of the Scorpio regeneration, rebirth, resurrection is indeed strong!

Perhaps the most important thing for you to deal with when facing life after a break-up or bereavement is the possibility of a seething resentment that it had to happen to *you*. You might find it hard to forgive yourself if you felt you were in any way responsible for whatever took place, let alone forgive anyone else.

The other thing which can happen is that you can once again bottle things up, building up a volcano of private grief within you which sooner or later will have to explode in one way or another. Go inside yourself to that private place within, to your Inner Self, and ask for help to ease your pain and enable you to let the aching and heaviness be lifted from you. The meditation and affirmation given later in this chapter will help you to teach your mind to calm down and switch off so that you can achieve a state of grace and tranquillity which in turn will allow your sadness to wash over you and pass on its way.

Of course, if you're a Scorpio you're not going to forget . . . but you don't have to remember the sad things *all* the time. Be that Phoenix once more, rising from the ashes, and you will know that life *does* go on and can still bring you wonderful moments too.

LIFESTYLE, HEALTH AND DIET

The Scorpio lifestyle is one which could easily go to extremes which perhaps isn't surprising when you consider that the varied occupations associated with your sign include religious leaders, surgeons, scientists, healers, criminals and those who tend to sexual perversions!

Of course there are plenty of you who manage to have perfectly balanced lifestyles, so please read on. It is, however, important that you have a *balanced* lifestyle. There is a tendency among Scorpios to experiment with life a little too much, turning to drugs and sex for stimulation, adventure and excitement. Alcohol could also become a problem for those of you who tend to become addicted easily. 'Playing with fire' is often a good description for you, and with Aids still spreading with no possible cure or vaccine in sight, and the incidence of drug crimes and drug-related deaths also increasing wildly, it is so important that you realise the dangers that may lurk around the corner. Even if you do insist on thinking of yourself as the 'sex symbol of the Zodiac', do at least remember to practise safe sex and try to avoid promiscuity.

Because you are so often interested in things of a psychic nature and are often possessed with considerable psychic ability yourself, you may be interested in learning how to read the Tarot Cards; and because the idea of reincarnation is also fascinating to you, you may decide to find a practitioner in Regression, or perhaps to learn about Rebirthing which in itself is a regression technique because it involves reliving your own birth and coming to terms with this. Massage is always something which appeals to the sensual side of your nature, and discovering the healing power of crystals will also fascinate many of you.

Of course there will also be times when you enjoy getting dressed up to kill and dancing the night away at a favourite disco! But your lifestyle also needs to contain those moments when you can cut off from the world and perhaps listen to your favourite music or meditate in your own special way or simply be alone with your thoughts. That is when communicating with your inner voice can bring you extra peace and happiness too.

Your eating habits can also lead you to excesses if you're not careful – too much alcohol, too many rich foods often late at night. And yet when you are in balance with yourself you're often the sort of person who can switch to a completely healthy diet without any trouble at all.

Scorpio rules the reproductive system and the genital organs in general; the bladder, urethra, descending colon, anus, rectum and the prostate gland. It is often said that you can have problems in these areas when you hold back your deepest feelings and refuse to let go of negative patterns. Scorpio also rules the nose, and nose bleeds are quite common with your sign. Your excesses can ruin your health so it's up to you – and also back to your sexual habits again. If you *are* taken ill, which isn't always that often, the influence of Pluto gives you amazingly recuperative powers, which are a definite bonus.

GROWING OLD GRACEFULLY

Growing old is one thing, but I'm not sure that gracefully is actually a word you would choose yourself. Don't worry, Scorpio – you won't lose your magnetism and charisma even with the advancing years. But you will hopefully have become less of a churning volcano of intensely emotional thoughts and even actions, otherwise you risk burning yourself out far too soon!

Knowing what it is like to have a dark side to your nature, you may decide that you're going to try to help other people less fortunate than you. Perhaps you'll become a hospital visitor, or write to or visit people in prisons who for one reason or another turned to a life of crime. You will probably start to read more, or turn your investigative mind towards studying something for which you never had time in your youth.

One Scorpio lady in her seventies even decided to take up Yoga, and felt it was the best way for her to realise her deepest inner potential, for Yoga has no age limit! And it's certainly one way for you to try your hand at growing old gracefully.

How To Get In Touch With The Inner You

At the beginning of this book I wrote that one way to learn more about your Inner Self is to think of it as a little child. As a Scorpio you could think of this little child as someone who sometimes thinks he is a loner, forced into a desperate search to fulfil his deepest emotions. By reassuring this little child that by rising above his basest emotional desires he really can hope to find the Nirvana he searches for, you will begin to understand your true self better.

In order to do this, your own particular form of meditation (see page 138) will be very helpful, for it will help to calm your emotions so that you can reach a tranquil and harmonious state.

Of course you may already have your own way of meditation. The way you meditate isn't important – what is important is that you recognise the benefits that meditation can bring to you.

Then each morning when you are washing and brushing your teeth, look at yourself in the mirror and affirm to yourself with feeling and conviction:

I will always use my inner power
for the highest good

The more you understand your Inner Self, the easier it will be for you to realise that one of your most important goals in life is to achieve the right balance between your higher and lower self and to turn any destructive feelings into creative ones. Meditation is one of the disciplines which can help you to do this.

The Scorpio Meditation

Choose a quiet place so that no one can disturb you. Sit comfortably on the floor, in a cross legged position (or, if this is not comfortable, on a chair), close your eyes and make sure you are sitting very straight and still. Allow your mind also to be still, but don't worry if thoughts come in. Just let them float on by, for now all that matters is that you imagine that in your spine you can feel the river of life itself. Feel this river flowing slowly up your spine until it finally reaches the point between your eyebrows. Then imagine that this river, full of energy and light, is bursting forth into a great sea full of cosmic light. Let yourself bask in the glow of this light for approximately twenty minutes, at the end of which time visualise the river slowing continuing along its path, the cosmic light now just a glow but its power ever present.

Try to do this twice a day. You will soon start to feel more uplifted spiritually with the realisation that your own life can be like this river which flows towards the light.

YOUR PERSONAL GUIDE TO THE FUTURE

By following the advice offered in this chapter you will begin to understand and know yourself much better, and once you do that you will be able to enjoy even more fulfilling relationships in your emotional and your working life. And you will be able to handle your own life better too.

It's not that you will suddenly change overnight, that you will lose your magnetism or that your sexual desires will necessarily diminish. But you will handle your strength in a much calmer, more balanced way. You won't use your power to try to possess other people but will use it in a positive way to do something really worthwhile with your life.

Your interest in the deeper side of life may inspire you to develop your latent psychic ability, perhaps starting off in a small way by guessing the contents of a letter before you have opened the envelope, or seeing just how many times you know exactly who is on the other end of the telephone when it rings.

Once you have learnt to let go of old negative thoughts and old ideas and are open to the idea of expanding your vision by listening to your inner voice, you really will start to be like that eagle soaring upwards in the sky.

When you have learnt more about your Inner Self and its deepest needs and desires you will be able to learn more about other people's deepest feelings too, and it will be much easier for you to accept that they need their moments of privacy, just like you!

The positive outlook you will achieve in your mind, body and soul will enable you to cope with those days of doom, gloom and disaster, and perhaps also inspire you to do your own bit to try to alleviate some of the suffering in the world.

Positive Outlooks

★ Using your energy in a creative way
★ Being proud of your loyalty
★ Controlling your intensity
★ Discovering the wonders of life
★ Enjoying your privacy even more
★ Soaring to the heights of success
★ Understanding yourself at soul level

Possible Pitfalls

★ Using your energy to destroy
★ Manipulating your friends
★ Forgetting self-discipline
★ Being too fond of self-gratification
★ Still denying others *their* privacy
★ Using that Scorpio sting
★ Hanging on to old patterns

For the typical Scorpio looking within can be something you fear – that dark night of the soul perhaps? But everyone has two sides to their personalities and doesn't necessarily like both of them! By getting to understand and know the Inner You it will be so much easier for you to balance these two parts.

Your own special voyage of self-discovery is your own special transformation to an even more fulfilling life.

Sagittarius

——— ☆ ———

NOVEMBER 22 – DECEMBER 20

Sagittarius is the ninth sign of the Zodiac, often referred to as 'the sign of the Higher Mind' or the 'Sage' or 'Counsellor of the Zodiac'. You are a Masculine, Mutable, Positive sign, the third of the Fire signs. Jupiter, planet of good fortune, is your planetary ruler and the Centaur with his arrow is your planetary symbol.

A positive, independent, optimistic, versatile, free-spirited and free-thinking, happy-go-lucky, athletic, truth-seeking, enthusiastic, adaptable, resilient, adventurous, generous, mentally communicative human being with a good sense of humour, a sunny disposition which is also moral and philosophical, an expansive spirit and a love of the outdoors – that's you. You're also known as the sign of long distance travel and most Sagittarians I've met put travel high on their list of priorities. You're always projecting your mind towards new horizons and new visions, searching for new vistas to conquer, and many of you follow that 'higher mind' description, being drawn to intellectual studies and philosophy and showing a keen interest in religion.

However, there is also a side of you which can take things too much for granted, especially the good fortune which Jupiter supposedly imparted upon you when you were born! This darker side leads you to become careless, extravagant, tactless, irresponsible to the extent of becoming too much of a gambler and behaving in an overly capricious and optimistic way. Your tactlessness can hurt people unnecessarily, for being direct and outspoken isn't always appreciated, as neither is your habit of moralising towards those who feel you should perhaps look at your own life first!

Obviously, in any astrology book one can only generalise, and perhaps your own personal horoscope contains so many diverse planetary aspects that your Sagittarius personality is overshadowed and nobody would even guess you were a Sagittarius. But that is only speculation, and meanwhile it's all too easy for you to come across as someone who thinks they can do no wrong.

It's not that you usually need to think about yourself in a more positive way, for invariably you are possessed with enough self-assurance and self-confidence to attain most of your desires. But because of your tendency to go over the top in your words and actions, it's important for you to discover how to balance your personality a little more.

Jupiter, as the planet of good fortune, can be a wonderful influence when you use it in the right way, for it enables you to smile in the face of sadness and instil a positive view of life into your own being and every one else's too. But don't rely on Jupiter alone! You need to create a better balance in your life as well.

All of us have an outer personality and an inner one. And in your case learning more about the Inner You can be one of the most valuable lessons you could have. Later in this chapter you will find your very own meditation technique and affirmation to help you to do this. Meanwhile, it will help for you to think of your inner personality rather like a little child, and that little Sagittarian child deep down knows he or she can sometimes be somewhat over the top but is willing to learn how to deal with it as long as you're a reasonable and understanding teacher.

I'm not telling you to suddenly change your personality overnight – as if a Sagittarian could be *told* anything anyway! But I *am* suggesting you make even better use of the philosophical side of your nature to discover how to lead a more balanced life.

Sagittarius is the sign of the higher mind, and you *do* tend to feel it's your duty to preach to everyone else about what they should be doing. It's not that you mean to be as critical as Virgo or as bossy as Leo. It's just that you genuinely believe it is your duty. In the same way, therefore, you can begin to believe that it's your duty to make your *own* life even more contented and fulfilling by creating the perfect balance between your innermost needs and feelings and those which make up the outer you.

What you need to realise is that while you generously want to share your visions, ideals and ideas with other people they are not necessarily always on the same wavelength or level as you, and this is why your philosophy of life isn't going to be theirs. By learning to communicate fully with your Inner Self you will learn at the same time to have more understanding of how other people feel, and will realise that by trying to insist on having things your own way you are only creating unnecessary difficulties for yourself. But don't worry, you will certainly not become a sheep following the rest of the crowd! You will always retain your own identity and be someone just that little bit different. Sagittarians who definitely retained their individuality include Laurens van der Post, Walt Disney, Woody Allen, Jane Fonda, Bette Midler, Sinead O'Connor, Steven Spielberg and Monica Seles.

Creating the perfect balance between your outer and inner personality isn't always the easiest thing in the world. However, as a Sagittarius that 'higher mind' side of you is willing to travel far in your search for the truth and for the deepest meaning of life. In that respect, too, Jupiter endows you with the belief that you can and will achieve your objectives, so that if your objective is truly to improve your life you can feel confident that you will succeed.

Any time you feel you're falling into the trap of thinking that you know best, even when deep down you wonder if you do, think about your opposite sign of Gemini whose mind is as restless as your own yet is always open to new ideas. There is always something of our opposite signs within us all, and something important to learn from them too.

Positive and Negative, Yin and Yang, we need to have both. And once you begin to feel the balance between the Outer and the Inner You, life in the 1990s will take on a whole new perspective, for you will begin to revel in your strengths and learn to overcome any weaknesses that might have sent you scuttling for cover in the past.

PATHWAYS TO SUCCESS IN THE 1990S

★ Use your ability to talk on all levels to strive for greater universal understanding and awareness.

★ Shoot your Sagittarian arrow to the stars but always be aware that you do have *some* limitations too.

★ Enjoy a full and exciting life crammed with interests but never forget to deal with necessary details, even if they do sometimes bore you.

★ Share your visions with those who also share your interests.

★ Don't just think philosophical thoughts: learn to put them into practice too.

★ Vow to be more adaptable and not quite so intent on going your own free and easy way.

YOUR RULING PLANET . . . Jupiter 'the planet of good fortune'. . .

One of the major influences on a male or female Sagittarius is your planetary ruler. Jupiter, which rules your sign, endows you with your search for higher knowledge and the deeper meaning of life. In classical mythology Jupiter was the great benefactor who represented growth and expansion on the Earth. The Romans considered Jupiter to be the protector of justice and virtue who with his qualities of wisdom and optimism was the most powerful of *all* the Gods. And to have this planet ruling your sign truly does seem to bring good fortune your way. Another name for Jupiter was Jove, from where we get the adjective 'jovial' which also fits your bright and bouncy personality.

However, if you haven't learnt to integrate your inner and outer personalities and have found no true path for your life Jupiter's influence can also lead you to become a dilettante and wanderer, trusting too often to luck to get you out of any scrapes – which is all the more reason to balance yourself properly.

Mythologically Jupiter was the Roman equivalent of the Ancient Greeks' Heavenly Father Zeus. He was primarily a Rain God whose function was to fertilise the earth, look after the wine harvests and oversee marriage ceremonies, treaties and oaths.

This Rain God had the thunder as his voice and the lightning as his weapon and was often known as Jupiter Pluvius (the Heavenly Father Who Rains). Another myth has him raised on the milk of a goat whose horns were overflowing with food and drink (which is where we get the idea of the cornucopia or 'horn of plenty'). Jupiter also represented prophecy, behaviour and morals – hence your sometimes moralising ways but also your ability to keep up an optimistic view of life which you happily endeavour to bequeath to others. And in Sanskrit he was known as Guru, 'the spiritual teacher or guide', showing us the principles of life.

The symbol of Jupiter shows the crescent Moon turned outward beside the Cross, while the symbol of Sagittarius is the Centaur, half man and half horse, shooting his arrow into the sky. In mythology this Centaur, Chiron, was educated by Artemis and Apollo, taught Jason, Achilles and Aeneas, and achieved fame as a prophet, doctor and scholar. The Goddess Artemis (also known as Diana, Priestess of the Moon) was an Amazon warrior huntress and her association with Sagittarius has bequeathed both physical strength and inner wisdom upon your sign.

In the body Jupiter relates to the liver and pancreas, and overindulging in these areas can lead to weakness. It is also associated with the hips and posterior pituitary gland.

Each sign has its own particular colour or colours and those most commonly associated with you are purple and a deep royal blue. Purple often relates to high spiritual attainment while the deep blue leads to a religious feeling – both often associated with your sign.

As a Sagittarius with Jupiter, planet of expansion and good fortune, as your ruler, and the Centaur as your symbol, you have a new adventure in front of you – a personal adventure which will enable you to fathom not just more of the mysteries of life but also the deeper mysteries of your own soul. This in turn will enable you to live your life to the full, expansively and courageously, without giving in to careless behaviour and overly moralistic ways.

THE INNER CHALLENGE –
THE OUTER CHANGE

There are bound to be some areas of your life which don't always work out exactly as you would like. And of course there are times when it's necessary to take a few risks too. But the trouble with being a typical Sagittarius is that in times of trouble you are often far too inclined to take too many risks without a second thought, blindly assuming that everything will turn out all right in the end. Just because you are blessed with having benevolent Jupiter as your ruling planet, it doesn't mean that you don't have to go through problems like the rest of us.

The following areas of your life will all be important to you in one way or another, so if you'll stop telling the rest of us what we should be doing with *our* lives and listen to what your Inner Voice may have to tell you the rewards could be fantastic.

RELATIONSHIPS

Anyone who thinks that you're such a happy-go-lucky freedom loving individual that you don't have time for love only needs to think about people like Maria Callas, Frank Sinatra and Kim Basinger who could hardly be called cool, unemotional folk!

Rather like your opposite sign of Gemini you can easily freak out if you don't obtain the mental stimulation and communication you desire, and it's true that you often find it hard to settle down. Your lover needs to be like a best friend too. You could also be searching for someone who likes the outdoor life as much as you, who doesn't want to tie you down in any way at all or contradict you when you are spouting forth about one high ideal or another, and who is always in a good mood. In other words you're being amazingly optimistic, and probably not prepared to see the benefits you can obtain from learning something about someone else's views of life even if they *are* different from your own.

Deep down you may yearn to be as dreamily romantic as Cancer or Pisces, and possibly even dream of cosy nights in front of a log fire. And if you're prepared to listen to what those inner needs are telling you a relationship may not only be a lot of fun on the surface but may also turn into one of those mind, body and soul relationships which you've read about or heard of from your more openly romantic friends.

The following guide will help you to see the benefits of getting to know that Inner You when romance comes along.

The Outer You sees Aries as almost as fun and freedom-loving as you but perhaps too inclined to curb your freedom; feels Taurus would never get past the starting post to fit in with your life; recognises Gemini shares your love of travel, and yet something holds you back; is much too inclined to feel smothered by Cancer's sentimental ways; could the preacher of the Zodiac cope with being bossed around by Leo?; intellectually you have a lot in common with Virgo but you definitely don't appreciate criticism; you enjoy socialising with Libra but sometimes the Libran lack of initiative drives you wild; while you're blatantly outspoken and honest, Scorpio's secrecy is just not on with you; at least you both know what it is to enjoy having a good friend *and* love when you're with another Sagittarian; can't you realise that your extravagance and carelessness with material things could send Capricorn running off?; you appreciate the unconventionality of Aquarius some of the time but perhaps not often enough; the romantic dreams of Pisces appeal to one side of you but only if you're ready to curb your freedom-loving ways.

The Inner You realises that fiery Aries is deep down a kindred spirit for you; understands that Taurus's dependable support could be just what you need to keep your feet a little more on the ground; sees that Gemini could be a perfect travelling companion in more ways than one; understands that you can help Cancer to be more positive while they can show you that being sentimental has its benefits too; is almost prepared to let Leo be the star of the show when you realise it could feel like party time most nights of the week; accepts that Virgo's criticism might actually have some truth in it after all; recognises the importance of learning to balance one's own inner Scales from being with Libra; appreciates that sometimes it is good to retain a few secrets like Scorpio does; agrees to let another Sagittarius think that *they* are right some of the time; your carefree existence doesn't have to be curtailed by Capricorn's practicality – it can benefit from it too; you learn from Aquarius that being a little more cool and detached can sometimes be a good thing; realises that travelling with a really romantic Pisces companion can be wonderful in a very special way.

By delving deeper into your inner being you will discover the benefits of stopping still and thinking before you tactlessly blurt out exactly what you think and of learning to communicate on every level. You will also appreciate in a more profound way that your partner has the right to indulge in a little preaching from time to time too! Since you are the sign of the Higher Mind you'll realise just what a blessing a real mind, body and soul relationship can be.

Learning more about that Inner You will also make you feel enthusiastic about learning more about the inner feelings of all the people who are important in your life, so that all your relationships can become even more rewarding.

CAREERS AND BUSINESS

Both male and female Sagittarians are without doubt among the most versatile and self-confident signs in the Zodiac. Good fortune often does seem to shine down upon you as you pick yourself up from what other people might look upon as disasters. Aleksander Solzhenitsyn triumphed over his years in the labour camps and Jane Fonda managed to avoid allowing the bad publicity over her political feelings in the Vietnam War to affect her movie career.

The urge to 'spread your wings and fly' could easily describe your feelings about career and business issues. You are often at your best doing something which doesn't have hard and fast rules, doesn't tie you down to a desk from 9 to 5 and brings you plenty of contact with the world at large. However, this doesn't mean that you are not prepared to work hard, and you are often keen to go to university and study for a degree in your chosen career. I have known quite a few Sagittarian workaholics, including those who have switched careers in their late thirties and had to start studying all over again. One in particular is now a practising psychologist, having originally worked in the media. Another has been a travel writer, fashion editor, gardening writer and accomplished artist, and now runs holiday seminars in Provence in addition to all the other things. Nothing is too difficult for you when you believe in what you're doing.

But your goal does tend to be freedom of one sort or another. The freedom to choose your occupation and your environment wherever possible is of great importance to the Sagittarian personality for you definitely prefer to live your life in an adventurous way rather than a way which confines you and holds you back.

Whether you're a boss or employee you still have that habit of being brutally frank at times when it would perhaps be best to think before you speak. Unless your chosen career really does happen to be as a preacher, always remember that too much moralising really does get people's backs up very fast.

You're not the sort of person who usually thinks about the long term benefits of a particular job; medical insurance, pensions, all those things are fine but you prefer not to think that far ahead and are far more concerned with what you're going to be getting now. You're not terribly concerned with money either, which can often go against you as you don't always handle it too carefully. You trust too much to luck, which means that working on a commission basis isn't often the greatest idea in the world for you. Your happy-go-lucky spirit and your optimistic view of life don't seem to let you worry too much about material issues. But in these days of businesses crashing overnight and high unemployment you do perhaps need to think more seriously about your financial affairs.

Sometimes you can waste an awful lot of time deciding what you want to do, procrastinating almost as much as Libra. One of the good things about communicating with your inner voice is that it will help you to use your intuition to let your deepest hopes and aspirations come to the fore, enabling you to balance your dreams of success with reality. It will also enable you to develop your inner powers so that you reach your goals more easily.

Being a preacher is one career which is often associated with your sign but others include philosophy, law, social administration, teaching, sport and sports promoting, politics, and being a travel agent, writer, publisher, bookseller or librarian. Your ability to express yourself also leads many of you to search for fame and fortune in the entertainment industry just like Frank Sinatra, José Carreras, Billy Connolly and Pamela Stephenson did.

HOW DO YOU HANDLE DECISIONS?

There will always be decisions to be made in life. The problem with being a Sagittarian who thinks they know all the answers is that you can sometimes make the wrong decision far too easily. It's not that you're as impulsive as Aries or as indecisive as Libra, but you often tend to think – perhaps because you've read so often that 'the lucky planet Jupiter is the ruler of your sign' – that nothing can go wrong. You also make your own luck by the way you handle your life, and you can't afford to simply rely on the fact that Jupiter is your ruler to enable you to have everything the way you want it.

Sometimes you have too many things going on in your restless mind at the same time and it's hard for you to think about any one of them properly, let alone make a serious decision. The meditation and affirmation which appear later in this chapter will help you to reach the still, silent place within you where your inner voice can guide you in deciding what you have to do. Remember that your Sagittarian Archer's arrow can only reach the stars if you aim it the right way.

Details often tend to be incredibly boring for you but you'd better remember that when important decisions have to be made you need to have all the details at hand. It's far too easy for you to carelessly overlook something relevant because, once again, you take it for granted that things will always work out. So often they do . . . but don't risk it!

How Do You Handle Conflicts?

Your way to handle conflicts is sometimes to refuse to let the other person get a word in! You can be so outspoken that your opponent is left slightly stunned, leaving you in what is supposedly the winner's seat. There is also an insensitive side of you which makes you so determined that you are right in whatever you're arguing over at the time that you can be almost as ruthless as Scorpio and decide you'll never see your opponent again! Of course you're sure to regret this later on and be quite prepared to forgive and forget (unless you happen to have a Scorpio ascendant!) but by then the damage will probably have been done.

While you have to admit you don't like to be challenged in any way, you also have to admit that you would rather have a carefree life without any conflicts than deal with unnecessary dramas and problems perhaps created in part by your own behaviour.

Since you thrive on being honest towards other people, perhaps you should also try a little harder to be honest with yourself and admit that your bouncy, carefree personality, with its inability to keep a secret or to accept that tactlessness is one of your faults, can create conflicts with people who take a more serious view of life. It's not enough to say that you hate pessimism of any kind so that a moody Cancerian had better watch out, or that the materialistic attitude of Capricorn drives you wild, or that you resent being tied down by anyone or anything. When you learn to understand your own inner being a little better you'll learn to understand and accept other people's positive and negative points too.

You As A Parent

You have a natural ability which enables you to get on well with your offspring, primarily because there is that wonderfully child-like optimism within your own personality. However, there is also a tendency to rather dogmatically tell them what you feel they should be doing with their lives even when they are old enough to decide for themselves. The lovely thing is that, deep down, you invariably do have faith in them – and heaven help anyone else who dares to say a wrong word about them. Even though you have an inborn restlessness and dislike of being tied down you don't often feel hemmed in when you become a parent.

Your children can expect to live a fairly free and easy lifestyle although you will certainly encourage them to study and develop their minds, and of course you will hope that they share your own visions and ideals. But while you don't seem to have a private side to your nature, remember to allow them theirs: don't pry into every little thing or upset them with a tactless remark, especially when they're at a sensitive age like the early teens.

Of course it's often difficult to stand back in these times of increasing drug and crime problems and with more and more people of both sexes ending up HIV positive or with fullblown Aids. But always try to be a best friend to your children as well as their parent. You will be rewarded by the knowledge that they will always come to you with any problems which might need your advice or help.

COPING WITH LIFE AFTER
BREAK-UPS OR BEREAVEMENTS

It's rarely easy to cope with life after a break-up or bereavement, no matter what the circumstances. However, blessed with your optimism and positive view of life, plus your philosophical approach to both the past and the future, you tend to rise above adversity like a born survivor.

What you do have to be careful of, however, are those fleeting negative feelings of 'why did this have to happen to me?' which seem to relate to the feeling that Sagittarians are supposed to have been born lucky. It's all down to that representation of Jupiter as the 'lucky planet' once again which has sometimes meant you have been overly optimistic at moments when more care was needed.

Once you've become truly in tune with your inner voice you will have more understanding about the meaning of life and how ephemeral it is. And you will know that sometimes you have to travel through dark tunnels in order to learn something new. Concentrate on your inner strength: don't aimlessly drift and think what might have been. Look forward to the rest of your life with greater faith, knowing that you really *are* a survivor and that life can still be an adventure if you believe it can. Use your special meditation and affirmation techniques which are on pages 156–7 to help you here and remember that, in the words of Paramhansa Yogananda, 'Happiness comes not by aimlessly thinking about it but by living it in all the moods and actions of life'. For believing that you will be happy again means you're half way there.

LIFESTYLE, HEALTH AND DIET

The Sagittarius lifestyle tends to be as free and easy as everything else about you. Many of you are great lovers of the outdoors, and even if you don't necessarily indulge in sport you will think nothing of taking the dog for long walks or going off on camping weekends with your nearest and dearest. A relaxing sort of life, with as few demanding schedules as possible and the ability to change your mind at a whim almost as much as your opposite sign of Gemini – this is ideal for you.

Very often you are exceedingly conscious of looking *and* feeling healthy, and some of you take your exercise regime almost to extremes. Not all of you are going to be Jane Fondas but I'm sure most T'ai Chi, Aerobics and Bodywork classes have a high percentage of Sagittarians among them. In fact most forms of exercise which involve getting together in classes with like-minded people are sure to interest you and you could easily be drawn to something like the Alexander Technique too. Sagittarians who are sports lovers can often be found on the golf course and tennis courts – Chris Evert is a good example. Horse riding may also be a keen interest but I'm afraid that gambling on the horses can also be one of your downfalls when you rely too much on that famous Jupiterian luck and discover that it isn't always there!

Then there are those of you who definitely go for the interests which appeal to that 'higher mind' side of your personality. You may decide to learn about hypnotherapy or psychotherapy or to use your 'counselling' skills to help Aids or drug rehabilitation patients. And of course you can be almost as much of a social butterfly as Gemini, enjoying discussions with friends and acquaintances ranging from the highly philosophical to the gossipy kind.

Your eating preferences tend to border on the adventurous although you are often a fairly disorganised cook in your own kitchen. Because you like to travel so much you probably have your favourite recipes from all over the world, and because you are usually such an active person you seldom have to worry much about putting on weight. You don't necessarily want to eat at set times but more as the fancy takes you. It has been said that Sagittarians especially need the mineral silica – a great muscle and tissue builder and an integral part of the skin, nails and hair – in their diet. Foods containing this mineral include cucumber, rye, nuts, cherries, whole wheat, carrots, figs, spinach, grapes, cheese and goat's milk and cheese. But if you're a typical Sagittarian you don't like being told what you should eat, much preferring to impart that sort of information to others!

Sagittarius rules the hips and thighs; also the femur, ilium, coccygeal and sacral regions of the spine, veins and sciatic nerves. If you *do* put on weight by not getting enough exercise and being careless with your food it invariably goes to your hips and thighs. Problems with the sciatic nerve also seem to be prevalent with your sign. Your ruling planet Jupiter also relates to the liver and pancreas and over-indulging can lead to problems in these areas.

I've often found that because you are always rushing about here, there and everywhere you can make yourself accident prone rather too easily. 'More haste and less speed' is definitely a worthy maxim for you to remember! Yoga and meditation are certainly worthwhile practices too for those of you who find it hard to unwind and relax your agile mind and your active body.

GROWING OLD GRACEFULLY

I don't think that 'gracefully' is necessarily a word which fits your sign. You would probably be offended at the thought that your activities are suddenly going to be curtailed and that you're going to be sitting relaxing in a rocking chair just because you've reached a certain age.

Don't worry, Sagittarius, you will still be sending your invisible arrows up into the sky looking for new vistas to conquer. You will still be keen to travel as much as possible, be as socially active as ever you were – and why not, indeed!

However, by listening more to your inner voice you will perhaps be a little more understanding of other people's likes and dislikes and not so insistent on pushing your view across as the only way to do something.

The philosophical 'higher mind' side of your personality may come even more to the foreground now, enhancing your interest in philosophical matters, religious affairs and greater spiritual involvement and evolvement may come quite naturally to you.

There is certainly no way you will ever allow yourself to become bored for there will always be something new in your life. One Sagittarian lady I know has just had her first painting accepted by the Royal Academy at the age of sixty-four.

HOW TO GET IN TOUCH WITH THE INNER YOU

At the beginning of this book I suggested that one way to learn more about your Inner Self is to think of it as a little child. As a Sagittarius you could think of this little child as your best friend, someone with whom to explore the world mentally and physically, and someone who has as much knowledge to impart to you as you do to him or her – an equal in every way. No preaching, no moralising, just a getting together of two kindred spirits.

In order to do this your own particular form of meditation and affirmation can be really helpful as they will not only help you to wind down but will also give you a certain discipline which so often you find hard to deal with.

The Sagittarius Meditation

Choose a quiet place so that no one can disturb you. Sit comfortably on the floor, in a cross legged position (or, if this is not comfortable, on a chair), close your eyes and imagine a deep purple glow suffusing your body, filling you with a wonderful sense of peace. At the same time visualise an arrow, symbol of Sagittarius, shooting love, peace and joy up into the universe, reaching higher and higher until it showers forth like a wonderful divine firework display spreading ever outwards into the universe. Allow your mind to be still, but don't worry if thoughts do insist on coming in for you can let them drift by. All that matters is what you see and feel. Let yourself sink slowly into this meditative state for about twenty minutes, at the end of which allow the firework display to slowly come to an end, leaving a beautiful haze behind it, and imagine that the purple light has imbued you with greater spiritual awareness and a sense of higher consciousness which as your eyes slowly open will remain with you.

Try to do this twice a day and you will soon start to feel its benefits in your daily life. And don't worry about the twenty minutes because you will soon know instinctively when they are up.

Of course you may already have your own way of meditating and that's fine. The important thing is that you recognise the benefits which meditation can bring you.

Then each morning while you are washing and brushing your teeth, look at yourself in the mirror and affirm to yourself with feeling and conviction:

Today I will channel my energy and enthusiasm
in positive ways to inspire all

The more you understand your Inner Self the easier it will be
for you to appreciate and delight in your greater awareness of life's
possibilities and options.

YOUR PERSONAL GUIDE TO THE FUTURE

By taking note of the advice offered in this chapter you will
understand and know yourself much better and when you do that
you will be able to have even more fulfilling relationships in your
emotional and your working life. You will also be able to cope
better in these changing times.

Of course you're not going to suddenly change overnight and
become a totally organised individual working to specific routines. Don't worry – you won't lose your sunny personality, your
idealistic view of the world. But you won't be quite so dictatorial
in forcing those opinions of yours on everyone else and you won't
be quite so tactless either! Hopefully, you'll be a little better at
keeping secrets (did you know that Sagittarians are supposed to
make hopeless spies because of that particular habit of yours, and
of course because of your honesty which you must *never* lose!)
and not quite so adamant on demanding freedom for yourself
when there are tasks you really have to do.

You may realise that your interests in higher knowledge,
philosophy and related issues can be put to extremely good use to
help other people cope with their lives – without forcing your
ideas down their throats, needless to say.

The wonderful thing about being a Sagittarius is that you are
always prepared to learn and experience new things. Learning
more about your Inner Self can be one of the most positive
experiences in your life and it will enable you to learn more about
other people's deepest feelings too.

It's all a question of balancing yourself in mind, body and soul.
And it's a quest that truly is well worthwhile.

Positive Outlooks

★ Having a relaxed and
  exuberant view of life
★ Developing your inner
  powers to become more
  creative
★ Combining philosophy
  and idealism
★ Giving more direction to
  your life
★ Really working for what
  you want
★ Showing greater
  sensitivity towards
  others
★ Realising routines do
  have benefits too

Possible Pitfalls

★ Being too laid back
★ Becoming too sure of
  yourself
★ Still preaching at
  others
★ Asking for too much
  freedom
★ Simply relying on
  luck!
★ Still allowing tactless
  remarks to prevail
★ Refusing to resist an
  unrealistic gamble

For the typical Sagittarius, looking inside yourself can be one of those adventurous explorations you thrive on: an exploration of your deepest needs and desires with the knowledge that your Inner Self can help you to land your Archer's arrow in the place of your dreams.

This magical, mystical exploration of the you beneath the surface of your personality will not just enable you to view the world around you will a more enhanced philosophical under-standing but will give you the vision to apply your own special talents and abilities to perhaps do something more to help others in the areas you know best.

Capricorn

— ☆ —

DECEMBER 21 – JANUARY 19

Capricorn is the tenth sign of the Zodiac, often referred to as 'the workaholic of the Zodiac'. You are a Feminine, Cardinal, Negative sign, the third of the Earth signs. Saturn, known as 'Old Father Time', is your planetary ruler and your planetary ruler is the Goat with the curling fish's tail or, as is more usually shown, the Mountain Goat.

You're a dedicated perfectionist and traditionalist; a disciplined, ambitious, hard-working and tenacious goal-seeker; a level-headed, sensible, practical, realistic, reasonable, prudent and reliable member of the community. And you often have a brilliantly witty sense of humour which can be quite a surprise to those who only see you when you're spouting forth with your somewhat rigid and moralistic views on life!

You tackle your life rather like the Mountain Goat would ascend a steep and craggy mountain, knowing that with determination it will reach the top. Your rigid sense of duty and valued sense of timing invariably mean that you *will* get to the top of your own chosen mountain, even if you sometimes have to navigate obstacles along the way.

However, there is also a side of you which can become ruthless, manipulative and power crazy in your determination to reach the top. (Astrologers always tend to bring up Richard Nixon's name in this context.) It's the side of Capricorn which doesn't care how far it goes or at what cost in its determination to achieve power and control. This negative side of you can also give in to pessimism, narrow-mindedness, superficiality, materialism, calculating ways and intolerance towards others who don't live up to your expectations. It's fine to be serious about life but don't be such an opportunist that you lose out on happiness too.

Obviously, in any astrology book one can only generalise, and perhaps your own personal birthchart would reveal so many diverse planetary aspects that no one would know you were a Capricorn. But this has to be speculation, and meanwhile it can be all too easy for you to come across as quite a tough authoritarian.

The interesting thing with you is that while you appear to be so strong and self-controlled on the surface, what you often yearn for is simply to receive approval from others. And often what you need to learn most of all is to start by approving of yourself!

Saturn, planet of limitation and delays, can be one of the best friends you've ever known, for it is Saturn who teaches you the meaning and value of time. Saturn's influence is there to stop you from rushing in where angels fear to tread and from making split-second decisions without sufficient thought. But when you become ruthlessly determined to pursue your own goals no matter what, even beneficial Saturn is forgotten.

We all have both an outer personality and an inner one. And in your case learning to understand the Inner You will be one of the most beneficial lessons which could come your way. Later on in this chapter you will find your very own meditation technique and affirmation to help make it easier for you to do this. Meanwhile, it will help for you to think of your inner personality rather like a little child. That little Capricorn child deep, deep down truly does need to believe in him or herself a whole lot more. And very often he or she needs to realise that getting to the top of the mountain and achieving material success is one thing, but without inner peace of mind and happiness material success can leave a very empty taste.

I don't want to imply that you're suddenly expected to change your personality overnight and become someone completely different. But it could well be time for you to direct some of your

Capricorn concentration on to your inner life instead of simply on your eternal quest for greater prestige, even if Capricorn does relate to the tenth house of the Zodiac which in turn relates to your status and standing in the world as well as career and ambitions.

No matter how brilliant you are at fulfilling your material needs, directing your energy to where you think it is most needed, or patting yourself on the back for all those times you are the last person to leave the office at night, you need to be sure that directing all your efforts towards materialism isn't making you feel you are missing out on something.

Learning more about your innermost feelings, needs and desires could be the shot in your arm which will lead you in a whole new direction and one which really could give you even greater security in the long run – security in the knowledge that you don't have to be up there in that Number One position in order to be liked and respected by other people. You'll be able to do what you want to do for a much deeper kind of inner satisfaction for yourself.

Fulfilling your innermost needs can sometimes mean a blind leap of faith, taking a few risks and doing things in completely different ways. But if you think of such a diverse group of Capricorns as Joan of Arc, Louis Pasteur, Anwar Sadat, Albert Schweitzer, Martin Luther King, Muhammed Ali, Federico Fellini, Ava Gardner, Faye Dunaway, Shirley Bassey, Annie Lennox, Gérard Depardieu and Anthony Hopkins, you will have to agree that they have all used their talents to the maximum, believing totally that that was what they had to do.

I'm not going to tell you that creating a perfect balance between your outer and inner personality is always the easiest task in the world. But difficult tasks have never put you off before, and indeed you tend to thrive on them. Besides, you spend so many long hours pushing the outer you ever onwards and upwards that it can be a refreshingly enjoyable change to spend some time cosseting the *other* you for once.

Each time you start to feel guilty because you're conditioned to devote your time to material issues think about your opposite sign of Cancer who knows the importance of feeling warm and cosy within. For we all have something of our opposite signs within us and they have something to teach us. Start climbing upwards to higher consciousness and you'll realise how much more positive your life can be.

Positive and Negative, Yin and Yang, all of us need the two sides. Once you begin to feel more balanced with the outer and the inner you life in the 1990s will give you even more fulfilment and security – and that can only be good.

PATHWAYS TO SUCCESS IN THE 1990S

★ Direct your energy upwards away from purely material rewards.
★ Remember Yogananda's words 'Concentration is the key to success'.
★ But concentrate on the positive side of life, not on the pessimistic 'what ifs'!
★ Learn to laugh at yourself when you know you are being far too serious.
★ Endeavour to balance your personal and your professional life in the best possible way.
★ Make sure you approve of yourself – and if you don't, ask yourself why!

YOUR RULING PLANET . . .
Saturn, Old Father Time

One of the major influences on a male or female Capricorn is your planetary ruler. Saturn teaches you patience, self-discipline, responsibility and endurance. In Roman mythology Saturn was Saturnus, the God of agriculture and the founder of civilisation and social order. To the Greeks he was Cronus, God of time and mundane time cycles. Saturn was Aciel, the Black Sun, to the ancient Chaldean astrologers and represented the sun at the midwinter solstice. The ancient Romans had an important festival, Saturnalia, which celebrated this period and many of its customs have contributed to our Christmas. However, during Saturnalia death and atonement were included and not simply joyful celebrations of the sun's new birth. Saturn also gave his name to Saturday which was the Sabbath of the week's end preceding the new sun on Sunday.

Saturn was often revered as a healer and the medicinal symbol Rx actually began as the planetary sign of Saturn. Believe it or not, this symbol was often written down on a piece of paper and then eaten to cure disease!

Saturn or Chronus was the oldest of the gods and as well as being the time keeper was also the law giver and task master of everyone on Earth. He was there to teach, test and represent the highest forms of justice and achievement and was responsible for grounding energy by relating it to the Earth and to practical issues. The 'saturnine' qualities such as darkness, sombreness, heaviness, passivity and coldness have been associated with him.

However, while astrology always does tend to call Saturn 'the task master of the Zodiac' I believe that he can and does bring the greatest rewards. Demands and limitations are sometimes necessary and they bring their own special lessons. Likewise, Saturn's influence on you can be more beneficial if you're prepared to balance your inner and outer lives so that the material issues of life don't take precedence over everything else. For then Saturn will bring you those rewards through self-discipline combined with faith in yourself.

Saturn takes roughly twenty-eight and a half years to go around the Zodiac, and when it returns to the place it occupied at your birth it invariably coincides with a highly important time in your life – sometimes even a crisis point, but always with an important lesson to be learnt! I've often said that those first twenty-eight and a half years of your life can sometimes be difficult for a Capricorn, and after that it all starts to become easier. It's almost as though you have to go through a testing period before you begin to reap those Saturnian rewards!

Saturn is often depicted as the reaper, the time keeper holding his hour-glass and scythe. His planetary glyph shows the same cross and crescent as that of Jupiter, but with the 'cross of matter' above which in turn relates to your own strong sense of material responsibility.

In the body Saturn relates to the body structure, backbone, teeth, joints, bones, skin and nails, and also the gall-bladder and spleen.

Every sign has its own particular colour or colours, and yours are usually given as dark green, brown, dark grey and black. Elegant Capricorn ladies really do tend to look stunning in black gowns!

As a Capricorn with Saturn, planet of self-discipline and limitation, as your ruler and the Time Keeper as your symbol you have a worthwhile challenge ahead of you – that of opening up to your inner being and listening to your deepest needs and desires so that these in turn are balanced with your outer needs for security in all its forms.

THE INNER CHALLENGE –
THE OUTER CHANGE

All of us have certain areas of our lives which don't always work out exactly as we would wish. And it is especially important for you to get your priorities right so that you don't lose something valuable in trying to achieve them. Perhaps it is unfair to mention Richard Nixon again here, but I feel he had lost sight and sound of his inner voice long before he got as far as Watergate.

If you're a typical Capricorn your feet are sometimes so firmly entrenched on the ground that it's the only place you feel safe. You don't mind how long it takes you to attain those material objectives, but you almost equate the idea of going within and expanding your vision to a higher place with my telling you to drop everything and race off to India to find the right guru. (Actually, Paramhansa Yogananda was both a Capricorn *and* a famed master yogi, author of *Autobiography of a Yogi* – and if you start off by reading that very book you will be on the first steps of a special path to higher consciousness.)

The following areas will all be important to you in one way or another, and if you're prepared to open yourself up to a more positive and optimistic view of yourself, and resolve to listen to what your inner voice has to say, the rewards can be never ending.

RELATIONSHIPS

Dare I say it? Do some of you set so much store on traditionalism, financial security and the right background that you actually go into a relationship with those very things in mind? Do you concentrate too much on wondering just how much your partner can be an asset in your personal aims and ambitions? There is a side of your personality which can make you quite an opportunist and fairly unsentimental at the same time if your status is involved.

Needless to say, you tend to be very faithful, loyal and dependable when you *are* in a relationship. Divorce isn't something you think of lightly even in these days of quickie marriages and equally quick break-ups. And you can be romantic too. But you're sometimes so determined to be in the sort of conventionally solid and financially stable relationship which makes you feel secure that you might lose out on fulfilling your true heart's desires!

Deep down you might wish you could be as romantic as Pisces or as flamboyant as Leo. Why not allow your inner voice to guide you and enlighten you so that you start to see the benefits of visualising the perfect relationship, and then turn that visualisation into something real? Even if you've been married for years you will probably find you can still learn to inject a little more romanticism into your relationship.

By delving deeper into your inner being you will learn to be less structured in your rigid routines and demands on yourself and on others. You'll start to like and love yourself for who you are and not who your parents were and where you went to school, and in that way you'll be less caught up in the material world you've tied yourself to so often.

By learning more about that Inner You, you will be inspired to learn more about the inner feelings of everyone who is important to you so that all your relationships will become more rewarding too.

The Outer You   sees Aries as too much of an impatient go-getter; finds Taurus much more sensible and earthbound; probably couldn't cope with Gemini's social schedule; thinks Cancer could provide you with stable domesticity; shudders when thinking of Leo's extravagance; enjoys Virgo's perfectionist ways but won't take criticism; finds Libra's charm and diplomacy almost too good to be true; is probably embarrassed by sexy Scorpio's sensual ways; can't cope with that free and easy Sagittarian manner; can hardly fail to appreciate another workaholic in Capricorn; conventional you with unpredictable Aquarius . . . never; doesn't always believe too much in romantic dreamers like Pisces.

The Inner You   appreciates the excitement which Aries can add to your life; realises that Taurus could be a very special soulmate; accepts from Gemini that learning how to be more flirtatious can be fun; understands that opposite signs truly do have lots to learn from each other so wants to know Cancer better; enjoys letting your hair down and having some fun with Leo; understands that Virgo shares lots of the same goals as you; sees that Libra could be a wonderful help in showing you how to achieve a better balance; resolves not to be fearful of Scorpio's sexual power, when you have your own powers too; learns from Sagittarius that a freer and easier life can have its benefits; promises Capricorn that life won't be *all* work and no play; accepts that a little Aquarian unpredictability could do wonders for a life of routine; visualises being as romantic as Pisces and watching glorious sunsets together too.

CAREERS AND BUSINESS

Both male and female Capricorns are probably the most career-minded, business-orientated, status-conscious people in the Zodiac. Your financial security is usually uppermost in your mind and you usually have the patience, self-will and determination to put incredible effort into succeeding at anything you undertake. Marlene Dietrich did! So did Howard Hughes. But you have to be careful . . . It wasn't just Richard Nixon who fell from power: think about Chairman Mao Tse Tung and John de Lorean.

You wouldn't necessarily think that show business was the sort of career which would attract your sign unless you'd had a personal word from heaven that you were going to be a big success. But there have been a lot of successful show business stars born under your sign, such as Humphrey Bogart, Cary Grant, David Bowie, Rod Stewart, Kevin Costner, Tracey Ullman, Donna Summer, Mary Tyler Moore, Ben Kingsley, Diane Keaton and Dolly Parton.

The more communication you have with your inner voice, the greater will be your belief that you truly can get to the top. At the same time you will appreciate the value of doing something you really enjoy and not just doing it for the sake of the financial rewards.

In the vastly changing world of the 1990s, when heavy recession is hitting people deeply far and wide, your particular business acumen is definitely a blessing. In the business world you can truly be a guiding light but it is important that you don't become so power hungry and greedy that you start to manipulate other people for your own use. Basically you are honest and just but the less evolved among you, who worship money for the material things it can bring, become much too single-minded in your quest for success – yet one more reason to go within and question yourself about what you really want. This certainly doesn't come from a jealousy of your inborn ability to make money, but from my astrological knowledge of what happens to Capricorns who concentrate on that and that alone. I can think of one Capricorn man who wasn't satisfied with his not insubstantial earnings from his everyday business life but even turned to gambling to try to satisfy his craving for owning more and more material objects. The result, I'm afraid, was bankruptcy. Now that same man is much happier applying his skills to something which might pay him less but brings him greater inner peace.

Capricorn careers include such occupations as business tycoons, politicians, entrepreneurs of every kind, teachers, statesmen, scientists, bankers, administrators, tax collectors, show business and organisers of all kinds.

Your outer goal may well be material success, and it usually is! But remember to give your soul security too for you will like yourself a whole lot better in the long run.

How Do You Handle Decisions?

Naturally there will always be decisions to be made in life and one of the questions you will have to ask yourself if you're a typical Capricorn is whether you are always totally true to yourself when you do make decisions. This isn't meant to imply that you tend to lie, but by being *totally* truthful I mean listening to what you know deep down is the right decision for you to make and not letting yourself be influenced purely by material, practical or conventional reasons or by the fear of taking a step into the unknown because you have never done things that way before.

One of the great advantages of becoming more in tune with your inner voice is that you learn to trust your intuition and discover what is really best for you. The benefit of Saturn's influence on you is that it teaches you patience and understanding, but if you're not careful and are living too much on a material level it can also restrict your thinking and influence your decision making by making you feel afraid to go past a certain point. Sometimes decision making does mean taking a few risks but unless you are very untypical of your sign you are unlikely to suddenly gamble your life away by deciding to do something completely alien to your nature unless you are very, very sure that in the long run it will work out and you inner voice will not let you down.

How Do You Handle Conflicts?

Conflicts sometimes arise with you because of your somewhat stern and over-conventional attitude to life in general. It can be difficult for you to bend from your rigid beliefs and sometimes you can be extremely patronising and almost ruthless towards someone who doesn't agree with you. And that in itself can often be enough to start an argument. . . .

When you start to look within, to communicate with your inner voice, you will probably realise that there have been too many times when you perhaps insisted on judging others by your own high standards or tried to force your own rules upon them.

That negative part of your character which strives for power and control needs to be balanced with a more open mind, with the ability to broaden your vision and accept that arguing is invariably a waste of energy on everyone's part.

It's all very well to say that the extravagance of Pisces drives you wild, that the unpredictability of Aquarius is unforgivable or that you're the only person who works hard in your office. If you really want to try to change the world there is no better place to start than by understanding your own shortcomings and trying to do something positive about them first, before you scream at someone else for theirs.

It's also important for you to develop that sense of humour which can be lacking in your personality for when you are able to laugh at yourself it also becomes so much easier to see a lot of conflicts in perspective and not make them into something more important than they are.

YOU AS A PARENT

Don't simply concentrate on providing material security for your children but make sure they feel emotionally secure too. I've often thought that Capricorns come into this world almost as little adults, with an old head on young shoulders, and that sometimes you miss out on certain aspects of childhood. But if that is how you felt when young don't pass it on to your own children, whatever signs they may be.

There is no doubt that you will be able to dish out all the discipline that is necessary as your children are growing up but remember that loving communication is extremely important too. Remember that if you continually tell someone not to do something without giving them a really logical explanation it only makes them want to do it even more. Of course respect is necessary from your offspring but let them respect you genuinely and not just because you demand it.

You can be an extremely devoted parent, often working even harder than usual to ensure that your children receive the best education and start in the world that you can afford, and you will definitely see to it that they respect the value of money. But remember to have fun with your children too, for by being their good friend as well as their parent you will be able to rest assured that they will always feel they can talk to you about any troubles which might come their way once they have left home and started their own lives.

COPING WITH LIFE AFTER BREAK-UPS OR BEREAVEMENTS

I've always said that people born under the sign of Capricorn tend to be rather like a good wine, maturing with age. Naturally, coping with break-ups or bereavements is rarely easy but there is a fantastically strong survival streak in your make-up which enables you to rise above adversity more painlessly than some of the other signs.

What is important is that you don't become overly pessimistic, feeling that some light has gone out of your life. Now more than ever it is important to communicate with your Higher Self, that still, silent voice within, and perhaps ask for guidance as to your next steps.

Sometimes you really may have to take a gamble, to contemplate a move or change your life in some other way. And you must never lose that sense of humour which hopefully has begun to develop along the way.

Always remember that Saturn, Old Father Time, does bring rewards to those who hang on, and continue to have faith in yourself and in your ideals. Sometimes it is good for you to be alone for in those quiet silent moments your inner voice will give you greater courage to climb higher up the mountain, just like that mountain goat which is your symbol.

LIFESTYLE, HEALTH AND DIET

The Capricorn lifestyle is sometimes dedicated a little too much to an austere regime of work, work and more work. Okay, maybe that is an exaggeration but there are an awful lot of people born under your sign who don't give yourselves enough time to have real fun. If you truly want to have a balanced life you will have to admit that *some* fun can hardly be called a sin!

Some of you will also probably say that your work *is* your life, and that you enjoy every minute of it. There is certainly no sign of Rod Stewart giving up his rock concerts and recordings! However, there are also many of you who don't have careers which take you here, there and everywhere and who deep down would welcome an opportunity to let your hair down once in a while and forget about your devotion to duty. But you've become so used to your daily routines and regimes that you've almost forgotten how!

Listen to that inner voice of yours and realise how important it is to balance your personal and professional lives adequately. Be healthy, wealthy and wise . . . don't just go for the 'wealthy' part of that little maxim.

The meditation and affirmation technique given a little further on in this chapter can be of immense benefit to help you clear your mind of the clutter of everyday life. Those of you who tend to spend your days involved in business of one kind or another could easily find a great deal of pleasure in those leisure moments you allow yourself by becoming more creative. You might enjoy going to art galleries or concerts or paying overdue visits to the theatre. Some of you might actually decide to take up a creative activity yourself. Yoga would be wonderful for you as it would relax your mind and body and be a great incentive for you to be more in touch with your soul. And I can't think of anyone more deserving of a good aromatherapy massage or a weekend at a health farm than a hard-working Capricorn! Some Dance or Music Therapy could also be appealing as both would help you to relax and release your natural flow of bodily expressions.

Your eating habits tend to be fairly straightforward especially if you are one of those conventional Capricorns who believe in three square meals a day and not too much cholesterol. Plain cooking often appeals to you more than anything which resembles too much of a gastronomic feast, but this really does have to be a generalisation. I am sure there must be Capricorns among you who would delight in some wonderful gourmet meals provided you don't have to think about how much it is costing – it certainly goes against your principles to spend extravagantly on food, or indeed on anything! One of the most important things to remember for those of you who are determined to remain workaholics while still trying to listen to your inner voice's admonitions to lead a more stress-free life is to eat a well-balanced diet even if you don't have time for those three square meals a day.

Capricorn rules the knees, the structural elements in the body, the spine, teeth, bones, joints, ligaments and skin. It is said that when you get too set in your thinking you can sometimes develop arthritis or rheumatism because of crystallisation. It is also said that Capricorn has a reflex action on the stomach (ruled by your opposite sign of Cancer). Because of the link with the skin Capricorns can sometimes suffer from eczema, allergies and other skin problems. Saturn is related to the minerals calcium and phosphorus which are required for bones, joints, teeth and skeletal development.

GROWING OLD GRACEFULLY

One of the lovely things about being a Capricorn is that you really do seem to grow old gracefully! It's the time when you feel you can reap the rewards of your lifetime's labours and when you will also hopefully concentrate a little more on pampering yourself and enjoying what each day has to bring on a more spiritual level.

However, anyone who expects you to simply sit back and let the rest of the world get on with things is only deluding themselves. There is probably no way you will let your skills of administration and organisation go completely to waste and some of you are sure to be found helping local activities in one way or another or doing social work. Since you are sure to keep completely up to date with everything which is going on in the world, even if you live in the heart of the country, you may decide that your own particular talents can still be put to good use on an even broader scale, perhaps organising large charity functions for some of the major problem areas where famine and disease run rife.

Material values will still be important to you but the more you have become in tune with your inner voice the more you will have learnt the benefits of expanding your vision higher so that you enjoy life even more.

But always remember that growing old gracefully is the time for you to unwind and feel good just for you.

How To Get In Touch With The Inner You

At the beginning of this book I suggested that one way to learn more about your Inner Self is to think of it as a little child. As a Capricorn you should probably think of this little child as someone who is too grave and serious, too concerned with what needs to be done and what might happen in the future; too concerned with the material problems of a world he hasn't even begun to experience. Teach that little child to laugh and play, to enjoy being a little child, to find pleasure in sunrises and sunsets and in the colours of a rainbow in the sky.

Your own particular form of meditation (see page 174) and affirmation will be extremely helpful to you. They will enable you to reach that calm and still place within so that material thoughts and actions don't prevent you from relaxing deeply and visualising how to make your innermost dreams and ideals become reality.

You may already have your way of meditating and that's fine. The important thing is that you recognise the benefits meditation can bring.

Then each morning when you are washing and brushing your teeth, look at yourself in the mirror and affirm to yourself with feeling and conviction:

☆

My spiritual needs will not be overruled by material desires

The Capricorn Meditation

Choose a quiet place so that no one can disturb you. Sit comfortably on the floor, in a cross legged position (or, if this is not comfortable, on a chair), close your eyes and visualise yourself standing firmly on the ground. The wind is blowing harder and harder all around you, but while the trees are swaying backwards and forwards your body is standing straight as a die. You feel the strength of the wind but you feel the strength of your own body too, and you know that this inner strength will always be there to protect you along life's journey. Allow your mind to be still, but don't worry if thoughts do come in for you can just let them drift on by, helped by the wind. Let yourself sink into a meditative state for approximately twenty minutes, rejoicing in the strength you feel. At the end of this time visualise the wind dying away and everything around you being calm and still.

Try to do this twice a day. You will soon start to feel more positive with the realisation of your inner strength that will always be there to enable you to rise above problems in your everyday life. And don't worry, you will soon know instinctively when twenty minutes are up.

The more you understand your Inner Self, the easier it will be for you to balance your life so that you don't continually behave like a workaholic, allowing yourself insufficient time for relaxation and generally being much too hard upon yourself.

By following the advice offered in this chapter you will understand and know yourself much better, and when you do that you will be able to have even more fulfilling relationships in your emotional and your working life. You will also find you can cope better than usual in these fast moving times of continual change.

It's not that you will suddenly change your personality overnight and become an irresponsible, freedom-loving extrovert instead of a hard-working and responsible human being. And it's not that money will suddenly seem less important in your daily life. But you will start to realise that there truly is a right time and place for everything and that balancing your mind, body and spirit means that you will be able to achieve even more of your heart's desires.

When you learn to expand your vision and your consciousness and to see things in a more open way you start to realise there is so much more you can do to help other people too, without the need to judge them or criticise them for where they happen to be in life. You will become so much more impartial and so much more sensitive too.

Discovering more about your Inner Self also enables you to learn much more about other people's deepest feelings. And you will find that becoming more positive inside your own personality will help you to create a more positive life around you.

Never forget that Saturn, that old Task Master of the Zodiac, really can be one of the best friends you've ever known. Enjoy the experiences which life has brought your way, remembering there are lots more of them to come.

Positive Outlooks

★ Broadening your vision
★ Realising your inner worth
★ Developing your sense of humour
★ Questioning more than judging
★ Enjoying greater freedom
★ Befriending your inner voice
★ Enjoying a better quality of life

Possible Pitfalls

★ Being overly pragmatic
★ Concentrating on materialism
★ Indulging in too much pessimism
★ Still being too judgmental
★ Hanging on to old ways
★ Refusing to listen
★ Remaining a workaholic to the bitter end

For the typical Capricorn looking within also means learning to let go of the past and being willing to explore with an adventurous spirit all that life has to offer you. By getting to know and understand the Inner You your voyage of self-discovery will not just bring you nearer to your goals but will help you develop the intuition to know which goals really *are* best for you in today's and tomorrow's world.

Aquarius

---- ☆ ----

JANUARY 20 – FEBRUARY 18

Aquarius is the eleventh sign of the Zodiac, often referred to as 'the Truth Seeker'. You are a Masculine, Fixed, Positive sign, the third of the Air signs. Uranus, planet of invention, is your planetary ruler (although before Uranus was discovered in 1781 Saturn was associated with your sign), and your planetary symbol is the Water Bearer.

It's almost impossible to give a totally accurate description of your sign for you are without doubt the most unpredictable and unconventional of all the signs of the Zodiac. You hate to fit in to any one slot! However, the adjectives usually given to describe you – apart from unpredictable and unconventional – are original, independent, idealistic, altruistic, unique, intellectual, nonconformist, uncompromising, truth-seeking, reforming, progressive, highly intuitive, talented, often very scientific, very friendly and truly humanitarian.

Those are all quite positive, but on the negative side you are the sort of person who though sometimes wonderful when we fear the worst can be quite a monster when you're expected to be sweetness and light! You can also be eccentric, a total rebel with or without a cause, far too cool, aloof and detached, erratic, irrational, absent-minded, unstable, too idealistic and dogmatically fixed in your own opinions and sometimes much too reckless. Sometimes you land yourself in unnecessary trouble because of your views or actions. Wanting to try to change the world around you into a better place sounds wonderful in theory, and it's certainly necessary! But it's the way you go about things which often needs to be examined a little more closely by going deeper within yourself.

One way or another you are quite a character. But obviously in any astrology book one can only generalise, and perhaps your own personal horoscope contains so many diverse planetary aspects that your Aquarius personality is overshadowed and hardly anyone would even guess you were an Aquarius. But that has to be pure speculation, and meanwhile it's going to help you to know yourself better so that you can contribute even more of your positive assets to the world outside.

Sometimes you have to admit that you do come over as aloof and detached, but this may be a positive effect of Saturn's influence acting as a restraining force on those rebellious and sometimes revolutionary qualities that can lead you into trouble. Is it really any surprise that James Dean was born under your sign, a rebel with as many fans now as when he was alive? Or that Vanessa Redgrave, Zsa Zsa Gabor, Helen Gurley Brown, Princess Stephanie of Monaco and Germaine Greer are also Aquarians?

All of us have an outer personality and an inner one. And in your case learning to understand the Inner You can help you a great deal towards making the best use of your personality, which can at times be complex and non-conformist but is definitely exciting too! Later in this chapter you will find your personal meditation technique and affirmation to help you do this. Meanwhile it will help you to think of your inner personality rather like a little child and to always remember that the little Aquarian child deep down often needs to be loved and nurtured more, and to realise that sometimes it is so important to let other people know that they are loved too.

I'm not asking you to suddenly change your personality overnight – although that happens to be something you can do of your own accord quite frequently! But I think it's time for you to recognise that showing your emotions more doesn't have to be a sign of weakness (though you certainly don't have to go to the extremes of Aquarian John McEnroe!) and it could enable you to have even better relationships with other people in the future.

Aquarius is the Truth Seeker of the Zodiac and the Humanitarian, and you really do care about the suffering masses in the world. However, sometimes you don't give enough attention to your immediate family, your dearest friends, all the people whom you think of as being close to you. Believing in truth, fair deals and equality is very positive but looking at the overall picture of something does so often mean you miss out on the small print and what is closest to the eye. You make me think of a passage in *Siddhartha* by Herman Hesse (Peter Owen Publishers) which goes ' "When someone is seeking," said Siddhartha, "it happens quite easily that he only sees the thing that he is seeking; that he is unable to find anything, unable to absorb anything, because he is only thinking of the thing he is seeking, because he has a goal, because he is obsessed with the goal. Seeking means: to have a goal; but finding means: to be free, to be receptive, to have no goal. You, O worthy one, are perhaps indeed a seeker, for in striving towards your goal, you do not see many things that are under your nose." '

Somehow you need to find a balance between your sense of duty to the world and your sense of duty to yourself! There is just as much warmth and tenderness beating away in an Aquarian heart as there is in anyone else's heart . . . and when you start to go deep within yourself you will begin to appreciate the joys not just of giving to others, often in an abstract or detached way, but of fulfilling your own deepest desires and dreams and making those people who are closest to you feel much happier with you too.

Creating the perfect balance between your outer and your inner personality isn't always the easiest thing in the world especially if you have surrounded yourself with an aura of detachment throughout your life and become so used to thinking everything through rather than allowing yourself to feel it. But if you start off at least by revealing your innermost feelings to yourself, thus breaking down those defensive walls which have enabled you to be so very self-sufficient over the years, you will be on the first step of a fascinating journey of self-discovery which in the end will make your life more rewarding and fulfilling. You will be able to help other people more too.

Positive and Negative, Yin and Yang, we all need to have both. And when you start to feel the balance between the Outer and the Inner You, your life in the 1990s will start to take on a new perspective. You will revel in your strengths and discover how to lose some of that detachment which has left so many people wondering what you really think and feel.

PATHWAYS TO SUCCESS IN THE 1990s

★ Don't just think idealistic thoughts – put them into action!
★ Use your sense of justice to do really worthwhile things to help the world.
★ Resolve to be less impersonal when you see it upsets those closest to you.
★ Start to enjoy expressing your feelings and enjoying sentimental moments too.
★ Don't be reckless when deep down your intuition tells you to hold back.
★ In your quest for truth always remember to be true to yourself!

YOUR RULING PLANET . . .
Uranus, The Great Awakener

One of the major influences on a male or female Aquarian is your planetary ruler. As you have read earlier, before the discovery of Uranus it was said that Saturn influenced your sign but since Sir William Herschel discovered Uranus in 1781 it has ruled Aquarius. The discovery of Uranus coincided with new scientific discoveries and inventions and Uranus is always associated with change, independence and invention – all characteristics which relate strongly to your personality. Uranus has been called 'the awakener of humanity to a new age' and its orbit is different from all the other planets for it lies on its side and rolls about. Uranus rules electricity and atomic radiation (uranium!) and its glyph, which comes from the letter H for Herschel, is two half crescents separated by the cross of matter.

In mythology, Mother Earth gave birth to Uranus, who became incestuously the father of all mankind when his magical urine, semen or blood came down as rain and in turn fertilised Mother Earth. He was also the father of the Titans, among whom was Cronus or Saturn who later castrated him! Uranus was also a western form of Varuna, a Hindu deity of indeterminate sex, while for the Persians he was 'varan', a spirit of sexual intercourse.

In the body Uranus relates to the nervous system and the electrical force which flows through the nerve channels. It also rules the pituitary gland and the saline solution of the blood and is connected with the circulatory system too.

Every sign has its own particular colour or colours. Electric blue is the one most often associated with Aquarius although violet, indigo and azure can also be Aquarius colours. Blue is supposed to help heal and relax the nervous system and raise the consciousness to the spirit realm.

Your planetary symbol is the Water Bearer or Carrier, a man holding an urn of water and offering it to all of humanity. But originally the figure was a woman and in the hieroglyphics of the Egyptians the sacred water jar was the symbol of Goddess Nut and of femininity, the jar representing the female genital organs.

As an Aquarian with Uranus, that great awakener, as your ruler and the Water Bearer as your symbol you have an exciting challenge ahead of you – that of retaining your humanitarian qualities and desire to seek out the truth balanced with understanding your own deep emotional needs and those of the people who don't necessarily follow your ideals or agree with your concepts. The balance between your outward actions and what you envisage inwardly, when attained, will satisfy you immensely and is therefore well worth striving for.

THE INNER CHALLENGE –
THE OUTER CHANGE

There are bound to be certain areas of your life which don't always turn out as planned. But as an Aquarian, surely that is what makes it all more exciting since you usually hate to conform to any sort of rigid pattern! However, always remember that turning those idealistic thoughts into actions without sufficient time to run them over sufficiently in your mind can sometimes lead you into trouble – we're back to John McEnroe's outbursts on the tennis courts or Vanessa Redgrave's outspoken political beliefs. In lots of ways timing is extremely important for you. No one could ever doubt that your motivation springs from genuine causes but your vision just isn't the same as everybody else's and that seems to be one of the hardest things for you to accept.

The following areas will all be important to you in one way or another and if you are prepared to slow down your active mind a little and listen to what your inner voice can teach you the rewards may be greater than you think.

RELATIONSHIPS

A relationship with an Aquarian is not always the easiest relationship in the world because you are such an unpredictable person. But you know very well that it's as simple as that. It is all connected with your difficulty in letting yourself go sufficiently and trusting someone enough to reveal that innermost you. The words 'I love you' are sometimes the hardest words in the world for you to express. But perhaps by going deeper inside yourself and saying 'I love you' to your little inner child you will eventually find it easier to say in the outside world as well.

Deep down your feelings can blaze with as much passion as Scorpio and you can be as sentimental as any Cancer or Pisces. Remember too that Leo, ruled by the Sun and ruling the heart, is your opposite sign and knows full well the joy of giving and receiving love. And since we all have something of our opposite signs within us, and something to learn from them too, remember that just like Leo you too can thrive on love.

The following guide will help you to see the benefits of getting to know the Inner You when romance is involved.

The Outer You sees Aries as a dynamic fireball whose exuberance leaves you dumb-struck; feels Taurus could be horribly obstinate at times; enjoys mind to mind conversations with Gemini; fears Cancer's domesticity could be too constricting; recognises the challenge with your opposite sign of Leo; definitely does not appreciate being criticised by Virgo; finds Libra charming but too much all over the place; isn't ready for all that hot and steamy passion with Scorpio; thinks life could be quite exciting with Sagittarius; decides that Capricorn's practical ways are just too limiting for words; might not be ready for that mirror image with another Aquarius; feels the romantic dreams of Pisces could be too wishy-washy for you.

The Inner You recognises that even fiery Aries has a vulnerable side; understands that Taurus could have reasons to be obstinate with you; adores the mental stimulation attained with Gemini; learns to appreciate sentimentality with Cancer; enjoys discovering what love is all about with Leo; accepts that you do have a few points which might need criticising by Virgo; learns quite a bit about balance from Libra; appreciates that Scorpio has a private side just like you; decides you can live and let live quite easily with Sagittarius; understands that Capricorn means well with all that practical advice; definitely recognises the lessons to be learnt from another Aquarius; often yearns to be as openly romantic as Pisces.

By delving deeper into your inner being you will learn that there are benefits in being a little less unpredictable and conforming more to what people sometimes need from you. You will learn to give more of yourself without holding back and being frightened to express your emotions. And you will be able to admit that showing love can bring you a great deal of extra happiness too.

Learning more about the Inner You will also inspire you to learn more about the inner feelings of everyone who is important in your life so that all your relationships can become even more rewarding.

CAREERS AND BUSINESS

Both male and female Aquarians are invariably drawn to careers in which you feel you are being of service to the world in one way or another. After all, you really are the humanitarian of the Zodiac. But you certainly dislike feeling confined or restricted by a routine nine-to-five desk job where you have very little contact with people for your boredom threshold is very low! You need to be motivated and have every possible opportunity to use your original and inventive skills. Your goals are not necessarily towards material success or at least they are not usually financially orientated for yourself alone. What you require is mental stimulation in your work and many of you will have gone to university after leaving school in order to broaden your minds and educate yourselves further.

Aquarius is also the sign of invention and the space age – no wonder men like Galileo, Thomas Edison and Lindbergh were all Aquarians. It's interesting to realise that three American presidents were born under your sign – Presidents Lincoln, F.D. Roosevelt and Reagan; Boris Yeltsin is also an Aquarian. See too how many of you have gravitated towards successful careers in the movie business. James Dean, Paul Newman, Farrah Fawcett, Jack Lemmon, Gene Hackman, Burt Reynolds, Mia Farrow, Oprah Winfrey, Zsa Zsa Gabor and Vanessa Redgrave are all Aquarians. And the Aquarian inability to express deep feelings was never better portrayed than by Aquarian Nick Nolte in the character he played in 'The Prince of Tides'.

Always remember that you are an 'ideas' person and that you also need to retain your own individuality even if you are working in a large organisation. You're wonderful at working on projects in which you wholeheartedly believe and often better at giving orders than taking them!

And always remember too that you have tremendous power within you even though you sometimes find it hard to direct your thoughts into actions – or, as I've said before, you find it hard to get your timing right. One of the advantages of communicating with your inner voice is that it will help you to realise that those flashes of intuition which you sometimes ignore are actually extremely important for so often they are telling you the right answer.

Your sign relates to the eleventh house of the Zodiac which in turn relates to your hopes, wishes and your aspirations. It is also the house of friendship. Your hopes and wishes invariably involve other people, as do your aspirations, and never more so than in the area of career and business.

At a time when the world is crying out for help from those with so many different areas of expertise and especially in the caring and service professions it is wonderful to be born under your sign. For no one cares more about freedom and liberty, about the suffering masses, the under-privileged, homeless, sick and dying than you do.

You'd be perfect working in the United Nations or Unicef but ideal careers for you also include radio, television, the cinema, science (NASA would be ideal!), politics, charity organisations, anything at all for the welfare of others, astrology, astronomy, anything involved with computers, archaeology, sociology, writing, aviation and inventing.

How Do You Handle Decisions?

Since you are such a non-conforming kind of person your decisions can sometimes seem somewhat unusual or erratic to the rest of us because they often appear to have been arrived at with very little prior thought, especially when you have acted on your intuitive flashes.

But apart from your brilliantly inventive mind you also have a fair amount of naivety which means you can all too easily reach a decision which leads you off on the wrong track. It's the kind of thing which seems to happen when you get so totally involved in 'doing your bit for humanity' that you can only see one side of something. It doesn't matter how firmly other people may try to question your ideals or even come up with concrete information which should make *you* question them. You become so firmly fixed in your own mind over the decision you intend to take that you can go blindly ahead making the wrong decision regardless of everything else. It's the rebel side of your personality which can also make you quite fanatical about your intentions.

Learning to listen to your inner voice by clearing your mind of everything and envisaging perhaps a cloudless sky, a landscape of pure space, will help you to find the answers which so often seem to elude and delude you when your mind is only fixed in one direction.

HOW DO YOU HANDLE CONFLICTS?

Because by nature you are a very gregarious person you don't really like the idea of having conflicts, especially with your friends. But having said that, anyone who does oppose your views will get the sharp edge of your tongue in no uncertain tones. Then there is the soap-box side of your personality, prepared to state your case and fight to the bitter end for what you believe in, just as Vanessa Redgrave has done many times. And of course you get furious when you see or hear injustice, and no one can blame you when you see the morals of the world going downhill, and suffering increasing ever more steadily.

Unfortunately, in your handling of conflicts you often seem to find it very hard to see reason in the other side's views or arguments and can become incredibly dogmatic. In addition, while you tend to treat other people in quite an impersonal way you don't exactly appreciate such treatment yourself, for you can be easily slighted and hurt by the sort of remark which you sometimes dish out quite thoughtlessly to others! And you don't appreciate being criticised by Virgo, or bossed about by Leo, though you can be pretty critical and bossy yourself.

When you learn to understand, like and accept that little child within you even better you'll start to understand, like and accept the people around you better too! It's not that you will necessarily change your beliefs at all. Rather, you will deal with them in a slightly different way so that there might not even be a need for conflicts: a rational intelligent conversation will clear the air in a friendlier way.

You As A Parent

No doubt you will want your own children to grow up as independent as you, and that isn't a bad thing. But unless you have Aquarian offspring of your own who will understand your own limitations over outward shows of affection, do try a little harder to let your children know how much you care for them. It's very hard to be the child of an Aquarian parent, knowing deep down how much they love you and yet wondering why they are not as demonstrative as other parents seem to be.

The lovely thing about you is that you will usually find time to converse freely with your children, with no holds barred, on even the most controversial of subjects. Of course you will tend to have your own fixed opinions but when you've realised the benefits of understanding your own inner personality better, you will be far better at understanding your children's views too.

You won't mind having the house filled with children and you will enjoy communicating with their friends of all ages. You will also ensure that your children have the best education possible so that they can broaden their own minds and visions.

Even if you still find it hard to be overly demonstrative your children will know that you are their friend as well as their parent.

Coping With Life After Break-ups Or Bereavements

Independent, freedom loving Aquarius – it *shouldn't* be too hard for you to get to grips with life after a break-up or bereavement once your grief has begun to pass. The trouble is that because you've probably spent so much of your life holding in your deepest feelings you can go through a particularly bad time when something does hit you hard, especially if it is unexpected.

Once you have learnt to open yourself up more by communicating with your inner being it will be much easier for you to let yourself go and cry when you feel like crying, rather than bottling things up inside you – which is rarely a good thing for any of us. This is one particular time when you will find your own special meditation contained on page 191 of extra benefit.

Once your natural grief has been allowed to express itself you will find it much easier to get on with the rest of your life and to accept that even an Aquarian cannot always change what happens in the world. You will find it easier to help other people come to terms with their own losses too.

LIFESTYLE, HEALTH AND DIET

The Aquarius lifestyle is hardly likely to conform to any particular style, regime or routine. It will, however, be sure to conform to the way you are feeling at any particular moment! Free as the air you breathe and free-thinking throughout your life, many of you will be drawn towards New Age interests of one kind or another and could well have experimented with drugs at some stage in your life. The list of New Age interests is endless – and it might be a good idea to browse through books such as *The Personal Growth Handbook* by Liz Hodgkinson (Piatkus) or *The Whole Person Catalogue* edited by Mike Considine (Brainwave Books). Meanwhile, you may think about studying astrology or the Tarot; discovering more about that Inner You by learning about regression or Rebirthing therapies; reading up on Jung and Freud; finding out all about Kirlian photography and Radionics; and learning something about Buddhism, Hinduism and even Sufism. The I Ching is also a form of divination you may find especially fascinating, and Yoga is often one activity for which you are prepared to follow an on-going regime.

And of course, if you are a typical Aquarian there may well be a fair proportion of your time which you devote to your pet cause or charity organisation by giving impassioned speeches at fund-raising functions and attending protest marches. While you're not necessarily drawn to active sports, we mustn't forget Jack Nicklaus and Mark Spitz.

Social activities will also be extremely important for you, whether it is simply getting together with friends, or taking time off to go to the theatre or cinema. Lectures and seminars on a wide variety of interests are bound to appear on your agenda, always supposing there is enough time in your invariably busy life to allow you to attend them.

The more you become in tune with the Inner You, the easier it will be for you to know which path to follow, for you will be instinctively drawn to what is right for you.

Your eating habits can often be as unpredictable as your basic personality. You frequently enjoy ethnic foods so that Chinese, Japanese, Indonesian and Thai may all be firm favourites, while some of you may be believers in macrobiotics or have become vegetarians long ago. You often love to experiment in your own kitchens and may be an extremely competent cook. But you're equally likely to be one of the first to try out the newest and most controversial diet if you genuinely feel it is going to benefit your health.

Healthwise, Aquarius rules the ankles and the limbs from knee to ankle. Often you suffer from weak ankles and, coincidentally enough, while I was writing this book a good Aquarian friend of mine was suffering from two broken ankles sustained in a fall. Varicose veins and hardening of the arteries can also occur. Aquarius also rules the circulation and it is important for you to keep yourself sufficiently warm in the cold weather and to feel connected at all times to your heart energy – remember that your opposite sign of Leo rules the heart. As I have said earlier, your ruling planet Uranus rules the pituitary gland and the saline solution of the blood and has a strong influence on the nervous system. Magnesium and manganese are two important minerals related to Uranus, both of which help to balance the nervous system.

As a New Age sign you will be drawn to Alternative Health. Homoeopathic remedies, Ayurvedic medicine, Reflexology, Zone Therapy and Acupuncture will probably all be of interest to you.

GROWING OLD GRACEFULLY

Growing old gracefully may not be the easiest thing in the world for you to do if 'gracefully' is the operative word, because there is no way you will cut yourself off from the problems and injustices in the world just because you are growing older!

You are sure to remain idealistic and youthful, and continuing to interest yourself in what is going on and trying to think of ways in which you can be of help is going to keep your mind young and active. There is definitely no way in which your life is suddenly going to become boring and dull, let alone sedentary!

Many of you will find you have more time to spend doing voluntary work and aiding local charities with fund-raising events. You will be as gregarious as ever, enjoying having plenty of interesting company around you as it will keep your mind alert and give you the opportunity to have those stimulating and thought provoking conversations which are so important to you.

Growing old gracefully is also a time when you realise that you can't be responsible for changing the world. But you can hopefully sit back and be glad that by communicating with your Inner Self you have been responsible for changing the negative things about *you* which didn't please you. It can also be a time when you appreciate the blessings of giving and receiving love openly and outwardly without hiding what you feel.

How To Get In Touch
With The Inner You

At the beginning of this book I suggested that one way to learn more about your Inner Self is to think of it as a little child. As an Aquarian you could think of it as a little child who needs to experience love in all its many facets and in its purest forms and who in turn will learn to outwardly express his or her own emotional feelings to other people. By showing this affection you really will learn to love yourself more too.

In order to do this your own particular form of meditation and affirmation can be very helpful for they will help you to focus totally on you and your spiritual advancement so that you can reap the rewards that are waiting there just for you.

The Aquarius Meditation

Choose a quiet place so that no one can disturb you. Sit comfortably on the floor, in a cross legged position (or, if this is not comfortable, on a chair), close your eyes and visualise that you are walking in space, that the air is crystal clear and that everywhere around you are myriads of crystals sparkling in the sunlight. Your body is totally weightless, and very quietly in the background you hear celestial music filling you with the most incredible peace you have ever known. Allow your mind to be still, but don't worry if thoughts do insist on coming in for you can let them float by; all that matters is you, and the vast space that you are transcending, and the infinite freedom which you feel deep within. Let yourself slowly sink into a meditative state for approximately twenty minutes, at the end of which you will feel yourself transported slowly to the ground.

Try to do this twice a day. You will start to feel even more determined to put your humanitarian qualities to good use to try to make the world a better place, and your idealism will be directed in a more positive manner. And don't worry, you will soon know instinctively when the twenty minutes are up.

You may already have your own meditation technique and that's fine. What matters is that you recognise the benefits which meditation can bring you.

Then each morning while you are washing and brushing your teeth, look at yourself in the mirror and affirm to yourself with feeling and conviction:

I will try to be less impersonal with my deepest feelings

The more you understand your Inner Self, the easier it will be for you to realise that you can afford to be more open and affectionate without losing the strength of your individuality.

Your Personal Guide To The Future

By following the advice offered in this chapter you will understand and know yourself much better. Having achieved that you will then be able to have more fulfilling relationships in your emotional and your working life as well as coping even better in these fast moving times of change.

It's not that you will suddenly become a totally different character, a routine-loving, meek and mild follower of rules who no longer has ideals or revolutionary ideas. It's simply that you will be far more aware of your own personal limitations and of the way in which you can get other people's backs up the wrong way because of the way you rush helter-skelter into battle when you have yet another controversial point to make. And you will be far more aware of the needs and desires of the people closest to you too.

Realising the power you have within your intuitive heart will enable you to do even more to help make the world a better place and your determination to work for the welfare of other people will become stronger too. But you will also realise that sometimes there is only so much you can do and that, while it is naturally important for you to retain your idealism, some of your progressive ideas may still be ahead of their time. You will learn how to be more pragmatic and sometimes more patient too, but the causes you believe in will always be very dear to your heart.

When you have learnt more about your Inner Self and come to terms with your innermost feelings you will also understand more about other people's deepest feelings. In times of change and chaos, crisis and coming together, your ability to help others will be magnified and you will feel more fulfilled too.

Positive Outlooks

★ Broadening your vision
  of truth
★ Learning to express your
  own feelings
★ Recognising that other
  people have their views
  too
★ Tempering idealism
  with reality
★ Taking your intuition
  from the heart
★ Getting to know your
  friends on a deeper level
★ Enjoying being who you
  are

Possible Pitfalls

★ Being too dogmatic
★ Still feeling too
  detached
★ Refusing to conform
★ Being too revolutionary
  in outlook
★ Never accepting any
  kind of advice
★ Still finding it hard to
  get close to others
★ Trying too hard to be
  different

For the typical Aquarian looking within can be something you put off, either because you don't want to know what you might find or because you think you have more important things on your mind. But by getting to understand the Inner You, you will gain the knowledge and vision to help you achieve even greater things in your life – and greater things to help other people too.

Discovering more about your own deepest emotions can be one of the most exciting discoveries of your life, especially at a time when old ways are disappearing fast, frontiers are being broken down and floods of people are needing more and more help. Progressive humanitarian help will be invaluable if it is offered by someone who is able to communicate in a real mind, body and soul way – which includes that inner communication with yourself.

Pisces

———— ☆ ————

FEBRUARY 19 – MARCH 20

Pisces is the twelfth and last sign of the Zodiac, often referred to as the 'romantic dreamer' of the Zodiac. You are a Feminine, Mutable, Negative sign, the third and last of the Water signs. Neptune, planet of inspiration, is your planetary ruler, and your planetary symbol is the Fish.

A romantic, emotional, dreamy, sensitive, inspirational, intuitive, receptive, expansive, impressionable, adaptable, somewhat secretive and kind human being – that's you. While sometimes appearing shy, there is often a sparkle about you which comes to the fore when you are projecting those creative skills which lead many of you to seek your fame and fortune in the world of show business. Liza Minelli, Glenn Close, Elaine Page and Elizabeth Taylor are all born under your sign.

However, it's also true that you often tend to see the world through rose-coloured spectacles. You may find it hard to deal with running your life from day to day in a practical sense, especially when romantic and financial issues are involved. There is a wonderfully caring quality about you and many Pisceans truly feel they were put on this earth to help those less fortunate than themselves. But it's so important for you to come to terms with your own vulnerability, and your tendency to empathise so much that you lose sight of your own direction in the world and become far too easily influenced by or dependent upon others. Interestingly enough, if you're honest with yourself you will have to admit that *you* also like influencing other people and sometimes making *them* dependent on you!

Obviously, in any astrology book one can only generalise, and maybe your own personal horoscope contains so many diverse planetary aspects that your Pisces personality is overshadowed and no one would even know that you were a Pisces. But that is simply speculation, and meanwhile you sometimes go through life seeing too many things through those rose-coloured spectacles and dreaming too many dreams which have no place in the real world. And when that happens too often you can become disillusioned and confused, searching for escapism.

It's so important for you to think about yourself in a positive way and to realise that just because you are the twelfth and last sign of the Zodiac doesn't mean you have to be the last when it comes to leading a contented and fulfilling life.

Sometimes you can be so shy and timid, so fearful of expressing yourself. Yet the influence of Neptune, your planetary ruler, endows you with so much inspiration and imagination that you can achieve a great deal in your life when you refuse to concentrate on your limitations and think instead of what you can do.

We all have an outer personality and an inner one, and in your case learning to understand the Inner You can be one of the most rewarding lessons you could receive. Later in this chapter you will find your very own meditation technique and affirmation to help you to do this. Meanwhile, it will help for you to think of your inner personality rather like a little child, and that little Pisces child needs to be nurtured, loved and encouraged to turn those romantic dreams into realities.

I'm not expecting you to suddenly change your personality overnight, and that isn't necessary anyway. But it is time that you used your intuitive qualities to do the best for *you* without sometimes running away from situations or being almost as indecisive as Libra.

Pisces is the sign of the romantic dreamer and it is wonderful to still have romantic dreams in a world which has lost so much of its romance and is fast becoming so ruled by technology that even

Valentine messages are sent by fax. And it is also wonderful to be someone who not only cares about the suffering going on around but who tries hard to do something about it too. You certainly don't have to stop being romantic but there is a time and place for everything and you need to make a resolution to become more practical and not to drift through life without sufficient motivation if you are truly going to be of use.

What you often need is to be more receptive to your own intuition and not necessarily so receptive to other people's influences; to have more faith in your own unique talents and abilities. You have an incredible ability to see a situation in many different ways and with many different ways to approach it. Use this ability well for it is something very special, and listen to your intuitive heart for it will provide you with the answers you need internally so that you can go forward in the world with greater self-confidence and sense of purpose.

Naturally, creating the ideal balance between your outer and your inner personality isn't always the easiest thing in the world. As a Pisces you are more than willing to do everything possible to understand others, to provide the compassion and empathy to inspire them to achieve more in their lives. And just like your opposite sign of Virgo you often worry far too much (for we all have something of our opposite signs within us). But it's about time you used a little of Virgo's critical and analytical qualities too so that you can differentiate between what is worthwhile and what may be a frittering away of time that should be spent on doing something for *you*. When you are able to see yourself in a more analytical sense you will be able to do a whole lot more for other people too.

Positive and Negative, Yin and Yang, we all need to have both. And when you start to feel the balance between the Outer and the Inner You your life in the 1990s will start to take on a new perspective. You will revel in your strengths and learn to overcome any weaknesses which have left you timid and fearful in the past.

PATHWAYS TO SUCCESS IN THE 1990S

★ Take off those rose-coloured spectacles and develop more discrimination so that you don't delude yourself in any way.
★ Don't be quite so receptive to other people's influences if you're not totally sure they are to your benefit.
★ Use your insight to learn more about the real you!
★ Always try to balance romance with reality.
★ Don't let fear of rejection prevent you from following your creative heart's desire.
★ Believe in yourself so that others will believe in you too.

YOUR RULING PLANET . . .
Neptune, Roman God of the Sea

One of the major influences on a male or female Pisces is your planetary ruler. Neptune, which rules your sign, endows you with both your inspirational and your somewhat unworldly qualities. The psychic realms, intuition, imagination and dreams, together with illusions, obsessions and hallucinations are all associated with Neptune. It also rules alcohol and other drugs and relates to the pharmacology of the medical doctor, the herbal healer and the shaman. So as you can see this planet has both positive and negative qualities! It plays a great part in the lives of those two Fish swimming up and down stream, especially since you are such an impressionable and receptive Water sign and since Neptune was also the ruler of the oceans. Its positive vibrations bring forth your inspiration; its negative ones can lead to illusory escapism.

In mythology the Roman God of the Sea, Neptune, corresponded to the Greek Sea God Poseidon. The powerful Neptune used his trident (a spear with three points) to shatter the rocks, to create or disperse storms and to make the seashores shake. His planetary symbol shows him standing with his trident. Mythology also says he created horses with brazen hoofs and golden manes who pulled his chariot over the sea which became smooth for him. Other myths say he was the god of navigators and all seafaring people. Neptune's glyph is his trident, made up of the chalice of the Moon superimposed over the cross of matter to make the point of how material reality transcends into higher consciousness.

In the body Neptune relates to the nervous system in general, especially the thalamus (the brain structure which plays a vital part in transmitting stimuli to and from the sensory organs) and those parts of the nervous system which respond to psychic impressions. It also relates to the cerebrospinal fluid, the lymphatic system, the pineal gland and the immune system, and can relate to diseases which are hard to diagnose and to addictions, schizophrenia and alcoholism.

Every sign has its own particular colour or colours, and pale sea-green and sea-blue are associated with Pisces. Indigo or blue-violet and violet are associated with Neptune – just think about Elizabeth Taylor's violet eyes for a perfect example.

As a Pisces with Neptune, planet of both inspiration and illusion, as your ruler and the Fish as your planetary symbol you have an exciting and emotional challenge ahead of you. Learning not to swim adrift but to go up or down stream at the right moments; to avoid losing yourself in fantasy and to use your intuition in the real world. In this way you will create the right parameters to truly understand yourself and others more at a time when greater understanding in the world as a whole is invaluable.

THE INNER CHALLENGE –
THE OUTER CHANGE

There are bound to be certain areas of your life which don't always work out exactly as you would like. But that doesn't mean you have to wallow in misery, self-induced or otherwise. And it doesn't mean that you should indulge in escapism of any kind at all! Once you learn to understand yourself on a deeper level, to flow with a higher consciousness, you will also understand how to direct your whole being towards the direction in which you truly want to travel.

The following areas will all be important to you in one way or another and if you're prepared to still your mind and really listen to what your inner voice has to tell you the rewards can be infinite.

RELATIONSHIPS

Are there any Pisceans out there who can say they feel completely fulfilled without a loving relationship in their life? Look at Elizabeth Taylor again and think how many husbands she has had in her life. And also look at Joanne Woodward who has been married to Paul Newman all these years. Most of you are searching deeply for the one perfect soulmate relationship that sends you floating upward from the sea into cloud nine, and Elizabeth Taylor probably found it twice – with Mike Todd who lost his life in a tragic plane crash and with Richard Burton with whom she acted out one of the greatest love stories of our time, both on screen in the film entitled *Cleopatra* and in real life.

But romance can be an illusion, and sometimes it's not always easy to live with that perfect soulmate. Sometimes, too, you fall in and out of love almost as quickly as Aries, not because a challenge has worn off but because the object of a great romance doesn't live up to your expectations. Perhaps if you could be totally truthful it is those very things you feel unsure about in yourself that you find missing in your partner.

Perhaps it's time for you to take the help offered by your opposite sign of Virgo, who can teach you so much about discrimination and analysis, criticism and the need to work hard at living life while benefiting from many of your own romantic idealisms. For sometimes your desire to be in love truly does delude you when you embark on a relationship, thinking it is the be-all and end-all of your life.

Deep down you yearn for a soulmate but when your romantic dreams are disillusioned you sink into a sloth of despair. If you're really prepared to love yourself more for who you are you won't search so desperately and deeply for someone else to love you. And when you're more independent inside you'll be able to have a relationship which has no illusions and yet still has all the romance you need too!

The following guide will help you to see the benefits of getting to know the Inner You when romance is involved.

The Outer You   sees Aries as someone too full of their own ego; thinks Taurus is fine on ground level but can't imagine being transported to cloud nine; fears that Gemini would tell you a pack of lies from start to finish; likes those protective ways of Cancer but isn't sure on a long-term basis; is swept off your feet by Leo but hates being bossed; thinks you're just too much on opposite sides of the fence with Virgo; finds Libra lovable but sometimes so slow in deciding what to do next; is convinced that Scorpio is only interested in one thing – sex; usually decides that Sagittarius is incapable of whispering the sweet nothings you desire; recognises that Capricorn can give you security – but what about romance?; has never yet thought an Aquarian could say the worlds 'I love you'; might fall headlong for another Pisces without a sensible thought in your head!

The Inner You   enjoys discovering that 'little child' within almost every Aries; remembers that Venus, Goddess of Love, endows Taurus with almost as much romance as you; realises that mental communication with Gemini can be blissful too; finds emotional *and* material security with Cancer; is happy to bask in the glow of Leo's love, even if there is a little bossiness too; realises just how much there is to learn from your opposite sign of Virgo; decides that balancing Libra's scales could be a wonderfully romantic operation; sees that the Inner Scorpio is also searching deeply for eternal love; accepts that Sagittarius has a wanderlust but has the confidence to believe that *you* could be irresistible; decides to show Capricorn just how wonderful romantic dreams can be; realises that Aquarius may have other ways of demonstrating how much they care; promises to turn romantic dreams into romantic reality if another Pisces is involved.

By delving deeper into your inner being you will realise that your emotions sometimes fluctuate too much from the highs to the lows. And you will realise that you, just like Libra, need to balance yourself more so that you don't give in to illusory sensations or attachments but appreciate the reality of yourself and the reality of life in a much stronger way.

Learning more about the Inner You will also inspire you to learn more about the inner feelings of everyone who is important in your life so that all your relationships become even more rewarding too.

CAREERS AND BUSINESS

Both male and female Pisceans are without doubt among the most artistic, creative signs of the Zodiac. While you do not necessarily have a great deal of worldly ambition there are invariably many careers in which you could become successful, contented and fulfilled once you decide to concentrate on reality and not simply on dreams. However, sometimes it is far too easy for you to drift along with the tides, lacking any real direction.

In the 1990s, when unemployment is so high and the whole economic structure of the world is extremely unstable, it is more essential than ever to concentrate on reality, for otherwise your idealistic and romantic dreams could turn into jaded and bitter despair and the tendency to escape into an illusory world of your own. Your goals are not usually to become powerful magnates or build empires, although of course there are exceptions such as Rupert Murdoch, the highly successful Australian newspaper tycoon. Often material security is not as important for you as the desire for recognition in your chosen field, although here again it is important to remember your renowned inability to be very practical and to ensure that you strive to have an income which covers your outgoings even if you do not care about being wealthy. Think again about those two fish swimming up and down stream and make sure that you're not a Pisces who drifts aimlessly from job to job, unsure of your direction or your desires.

Emotionally, you are definitely someone who needs to feel you are doing what you truly want for then you become one with that work, using your imagination and inspiration to the full. Because you are such a sensitive soul it is also important that you feel at home in your working surroundings and not misunderstood or put down by anyone.

Generally it is the arts which appeal to you more than the sciences, and careers often associated with your sign include writing, poetry, acting, painting, music, dance (Rudolph Nureyev was a Pisces), healing, psychic work, nursing, social work, sailing, photography (Lord Snowdon was born under your sign) and the priesthood. Throughout history, famous names in the arts have been associated with your sign. Michelangelo, Renoir, Chopin, Elizabeth Barret Browning, John Steinbeck and Victor Hugo were all Pisceans. So too were Albert Einstein and George Washington. Michael Caine, Nina Simone, Miranda Richardson and Bruce Willis are among modern day Pisceans.

Because you do have such insight into how other people tend to feel and because you are so creative, it's important that you utilise both of these assets in your working life. That is why all fields of teaching and health are often especially appealing to many of you. It is often said that many of you truly feel that you were born to heal and to serve others and that self-giving is your true role in life.

Pisces relates to the twelfth house of the Zodiac, known as the House of Secrets – secrets which you keep hidden from the rest of the world and perhaps even from yourself! By going deep within and listening to your inner voice you will have an opportunity to discover what you truly yearn for at the deepest soul level. You may thus realise that you have unfulfilled ambitions which you would like to achieve and which may have lain dormant, perhaps through fear of failure or simply because you have lacked the impetus to do something positive about them.

The wonderful thing about being in touch with your Inner Self is that your intuition will be magnified and you will see how to turn your visions and dreams into reality.

How Do You Handle Decisions?

There will always be decisions to be made in life but if you are a typical Pisces you will often do your best to escape them, either by being exceedingly indecisive or by stalling for time on one pretext or another. With your inherent ability to empathise with other people's feelings, there are also many times when you find it genuinely hard to make a decision if it is going to affect someone else in an adverse way. Because the really evolved Pisces always is devoted to helping others it can sometimes be difficult for you to put yourself first.

This is why it is so important to find ways to clear your mind and allow your intuitive heart to bring you the answers which at the deepest level of your soul will always be there for you. Your special meditation technique and affirmation described later in this chapter will help.

Never be forced into a decision which deep down you know is wrong for you simply because you feel you have to do it. And don't allow other people to confuse or delude you by not bothering to have any necessary details at your disposal. You can be far too impressionable at times but with that twelfth house of secrets, which is also known as the house of 'one's own undoing', ruling Pisces it is important for you to confide in the Inner You and be guided by the soul level advice you receive.

How Do You Handle Conflicts?

Both decision making and handling conflicts will be greatly helped by listening to what your inner voice is telling you.

Conflicts are something which can often disturb you greatly for your sensitive nature abhors raised voices and unpleasant scenes and atmospheres. However, it is important that you know how to deal with them without turning to escapist tactics which so often only create a delay.

Because you are so sensitive to other people's feelings you should invariably know just how far to go to avoid arguments of your own making. But you also have a natural talent for acting and there is a negative side of your personality which knows just how to manipulate people to get your own way.

You also have to admit that sometimes you do over-react to people and situations in a too sensitive way. Leos can't necessarily help being bossy and flamboyant, and you can't blame an impatient Aries for trying to hurry you along when you're floating in one of your little dream states and there is important work to be done. Since you do have the ability to understand other people's lives you also have to understand that there are obviously reasons for the way they behave as they do. And it is this very understanding which gives you a head start on the rest of us in being able to avoid conflicts before they start.

Conflicts in the world, especially in these changing times, occur with never ending relentlessness. Sometimes great and sometimes small, there are so many of them which could be avoided with a little more awareness and understanding from everyone. You have those capacities within you so at least you have the ability to avoid conflicts of your own.

YOU AS A PARENT

As a parent you have a natural affinity with children and will give your heart gladly to do everything you possibly can to ensure they grow up in an atmosphere of love and happiness, no matter what sacrifices this might entail. You're the sort of person who will willingly adopt or be a foster-parent, baby-sit for your friends when no one else is available and read bed-time stories to your toddlers even if it means missing your favourite programme on TV.

Your intuition will enable you to know what your children are thinking almost without them having to say a word. And while you tend to be unworldly in many ways you are well aware of the problems awaiting unsuspecting and naive children growing up in a world where drugs, Aids, sexual abuse and kidnappings appear to be increasing all the time. You will always make sure they know how to cope with that very first day at school and that you're on hand to talk over any emotional problems as they are growing older.

One of your greatest strengths as a parent is your empathy. But do make sure you also teach your children the importance of understanding about money and other material issues so that they are able to face the world with a complete knowledge of what life is all about.

Coping With Life After Break-ups Or Bereavements

Soft, sensitive Pisces, always looking for that rainbow in the sky. Sometimes it is exceedingly hard for you to deal with break-ups or bereavements, especially if they are unexpected or have entailed your looking after a sick person who has been so much a part of your life for a long time. For although you deeply believe in devoting your life to helping other people you are sometimes incredibly bad at helping yourself.

At times like this it is more important than ever for you to reach that still, silent place within you, to communicate with your Higher Self, your inner voice, that little child within and to let your feelings flow outwards. Here again you will find the meditation technique and affirmation given on pages 208–9 of benefit. This is a time when it really is necessary to flow with the tide of life for there are some situations you simply cannot control or change.

Don't try to retreat into a shadowy world, using alcohol or even drugs to escape the pain you feel. Remember that there is something to be learnt from every experience in life, and by communicating deeply with the Inner You you will learn to grow stronger day by day.

Lifestyle, Health And Diet

The Pisces lifestyle fluctuates and changes as often as your moods. Somehow you seem to drift into a way of life and drift out of it almost overnight. You have to deeply feel everything you do and at times a lot of what you do depends on your current romantic situation – which means that if you're not happy emotionally you can sometimes sink into an abyss of depression. Therefore, this is the right moment to remind you that more Pisceans than any other sign turn to alcohol and drugs as a way out, an escape from feeling sadness or despair. Even social drinking can sometimes lead you to become addicted all too easily so it is vitally important that by getting in touch with your Higher Self you realise that learning to turn your life around and be happy again can only come from within you. Once you have learned to love yourself and enjoy who you are you won't be nearly so inclined to search for the crock of gold in a love affair you probably knew from the start was doomed. Besides, when you listen to your Inner Voice, you won't even feel the need to start the relationship!

However, there are so many things you *do* enjoy in life that your lifestyle can be wonderful. With your symbol of the Fish you are often drawn to water sports, swimming in particular, although the lazier among you are happy to sit by a river bank listening to a favourite sonata on your walkman or walking along a moonlit shore with a special person by your side. Artistic pursuits often appeal to you, whether it be music, poetry, acting or the ballet, and you often throw yourself wholeheartedly into doing some charity or social work.

Because you are such a gentle and sensitive soul it's important for you to have a lifestyle that doesn't contain too many pressures. And it is definitely necessary for you to have sufficient sleep as there is something in your make-up which seems to make you suffer tiredness more than most of the other signs. Because of your interest in psychic and mystical things you may be drawn to learning more about the Tarot or I Ching, Numerology, Palmistry, Zen, Reincarnation, Dream Interpretation, Spiritual Healing or Crystals. And since Pisces rules the feet, Foot Reflexology could be just the thing to make you feel wonderful. Some of you may also want to learn more about the Eastern traditions of Buddhism, Hinduism or Sufism too, while Yoga and Meditation will bring you great benefits.

Your eating habits also depend on the way you feel emotionally. When you're in or out of love you might eat either too much or not enough! And if you are depressed you don't always eat as healthily as you should. You tend to drink a lot of liquid and can even sometimes suffer from water retention. Again, it's advisable for you to steer clear of very much alcohol as it really does tend to have an adverse and often addictive effect.

Astrologically, Pisces rules the feet and toes and some of you may sometimes suffer from gout, corns, bunions and other problems related to your feet. You should always make sure you wear shoes that are comfortable and well-fitting. Pisces also rules the lymphatic system and it is said that when you hold back your emotions your lymph system can become congested, which in turn can give rise to swollen lymph glands and nodes. Because of your fluctuating emotions, it is very important that you don't get involved in any negative spiritual or mediumistic activities as these would also have a bad effect on you.

GROWING OLD GRACEFULLY

Growing old gracefully for you will hopefully mean that by now you have decided whether you are indeed swimming upstream or down, and that you have traded your rose-coloured spectacles for a clearer, more lucid view of the world through making greater use of your intuition.

Of course you will still be a romantic in lots of ways but the direction in which you flow will be one which fits in with the real world and the very real changes which are taking place.

Your desire to help other people may well become even greater and you will probably be determined to spend some of your free time involved in doing something constructive which does indeed aid those less fortunate than yourself.

Since you will have more free time on your hands you may also decide to develop any artistic talent such as painting. And it's never too late to join a local amateur dramatic society so that you can show off your inherent performing skills.

Growing old gracefully is a time to achieve the right balance in your life, when the Outer and the Inner You are perfectly in tune and when the question of whether to float upstream or down is no longer a problem, for you know where you are meant to be.

HOW TO GET IN TOUCH
WITH THE INNER YOU

At the beginning of this book I suggested that one way to learn more about your Inner Self is to think of it as a little child. As a Pisces you could think of this little child as someone who is so impressionable and sensitive to outside influences that he or she needs to trust even more in that heartfelt intuition which is part of every Piscean.

In order to do this your own particular form of meditation can be very helpful as it will help to still that flow of thoughts, impressions and sounds endlessly slipping by, sometimes without sufficient meaning. It will enable you to flow in the right direction towards what life has to offer.

The Pisces Meditation

Sit comfortably on the floor, in a cross legged position (or, if this is not comfortable, on a chair), close your eyes and, since you are a Water sign, try to visualise yourself sitting or standing in water, allowing it to flow around you and letting your mind and body gradually relax and become totally restful. Don't worry about thoughts passing through your mind, but let them slip by like the flowing water. Let yourself sink slowly into a meditative state for approximately twenty minutes, and feel yourself flowing with the tide of life spreading limitless compassion, warmth and love to all human beings everywhere, releasing any feelings of doubt or negativity. Then gradually visualise yourself back on dry land feeling calm and purposeful.

Try to do this twice a day. You will soon start to discover greater feelings of empathy towards others with at the same time a greater belief in your contribution to helping make the world a better place. And don't worry, you will soon know instinctively when twenty minutes are up.

You may already have your own way of meditating and that's fine. The important thing is that you recognise the benefits which meditation can bring you.

Then each morning when you are washing and brushing your teeth, look at yourself in the mirror and affirm to yourself with feelings and conviction:

The direction I flow in life will enable me
to do the best for myself and others

The more you understand your Inner Self, the more you will understand your need for that particular spiritual strength which will enable you to give your wonderful warmth and compassion to others without taking too much toll on your own emotions and thus taking away your own power.

YOUR PERSONAL GUIDE TO THE FUTURE

By following the advice offered in this chapter you will understand and know yourself much better. Once you do that you will be able to have more fulfilling relationships in your emotional and your working life and be able to cope better in these fast moving and changing times. It's not that you will suddenly change overnight and become an unfeeling go-getter instead of a romantic idealist or turn into a whizz-kid where finances are concerned. But you won't suffer from so much confusion and delusion in your practical and your romantic life for you will be able to see yourself and your aims and aspirations so much more clearly.

You have a talent to play many parts well but the more you have become in tune with your inner voice the more convinced you will become of the path you want to follow. 'Born to heal and born to serve' – in one way or another you will truly fulfil those words and do everything possible to ensure that those who are suffering have your love, your blessings and your help wherever it is possible.

When you have learnt more about your Inner Self you will discover you have learnt much more about other people's deepest feelings too. Balancing yourself in mind, body and soul means that even when chaos and crisis prevail in the world around you, you certainly won't be floating this way and that. You will be doing everything in your power to turn the positive aspects of your character to optimum use.

Positive Outlooks

★ Flowing towards greater enlightenment
★ Focusing on the positive
★ Appreciating the reality of what life has to offer
★ Turning dreams into reality and romance into reality too
★ Empathising without losing sight of *you*
★ Realising just how much you have to give!

Possible Pitfalls

★ Still drifting down-stream too often
★ Allowing negatives to impinge
★ Searching for an escape valve if things get tough
★ Sinking into a fantasy world
★ Losing your head when love beckons
★ Worrying too much about others
★ Undervaluing yourself and your talents

For the typical Pisces looking within can be a journey to a wonderful world of enlightenment where the knowledge bequeathed to you will enable you to know which is the right direction in which to swim.

You will achieve greater faith, serenity and self-confidence too which in turn will enable you to help in more positive and practical ways to give faith, serenity, confidence *and* practical help to other people.